MAGIC MINUTES

Quick Read-Alouds for Every Day

PAT NELSON

Illustrated by
Kath B. Gordon

LIBRARIES UNLIMITED, INC.
Englewood, Colorado
1993

For my grandchildren,
Abram, Eli, and Emily Smith,
may they always enjoy stories.

LIBRARIES UNLIMITED, INC.
P.O. Box 6633
Englewood, CO 80155-6633
1-800-237-6124

Library of Congress Cataloging-in-Publication Data

Nelson, Pat, 1925-
    Magic minutes : quick read-alouds for every day / Pat Nelson ;
illustrated by Kath B. Gordon.
    xv, 151 p. 17x25 cm.
    Includes index.
    ISBN 0-87287-996-8
    1. Tales. 2. Seasons--Folklore. 3. Storytelling. I. Gordon,
Kath B. II. Title.
GR67.N45   1993
398.27--dc20
                                                  92-35887
                                                   CIP

CONTENTS

OCTOBER (continued)

NOVEMBER

DECEMBER

JANUARY

FEBRUARY

FEBRUARY (continued)

MARCH

APRIL

MAY

SUMMER

ACKNOWLEDGMENTS

Grateful acknowledgment is made to the following for permission to reprint and adapt from previously published material. (In the case of adaptation, the author may have retitled the tale.) "The Women Who Canned 200 Jars of Turkey" and "Free Pepsi Cola" from *All Hell Broke Loose*, © William H. Hull, 1985, ISBN 0-939330-01-6, reprinted by special permission, may not be copied further; "Andrew Saves the Day," by Jerry Howard, © 1988, published in *Sanctuary Magazine*, December 1988; "The Laughing President" from *Treasury of American Folklore*, by B. A. Botkin, published by Jovanovich, © 1944; "The Sun Never Sets on Kitty" from *Book of Facts*, © 1987, published by The Reader's Digest Association, Inc., reprinted by permission; "Small Talk" and "Family Affair" from *Facts and Fallacies*, © 1988, published by The Reader's Digest Association, Inc., reprinted by permission; *Tales of a Chinese Grandmother*, by Frances Carpenter, © Charles E. Tuttle Co., Inc. of Tokyo, Japan; "The Sun Gazer," "How the Rainbow Came to Be," "Why the Baby Deer Wears Spots," "How the Ducks Got Their Colors," and "Why the Leaves Fall" are adapted from *Legends of the Mighty Sioux*, compiled by the Workers of the South Dakota Writers' Project (WPA), © 1941 by South Dakota Department of Public Instruction, used with permission of Albert Whitman & Company; *Pleasant Journeys*, Vol. 2, page 37, © Pleasant deSpain, 1979, published by The Writing Works, Inc.; "Sausalito's Hum Won't Go Away," by David Perinan, Science Editor, *San Francisco Chronicle*, final edition, News section, August 20, 1985; "The Childs Park Children," by Ann Loudon, from *Sanctuary Magazine*, April 1990, page 8.

INTRODUCTION

I was a storyteller performing in classrooms when I discovered teachers live and die for minutes. They are always looking for something to fill the time between classes or subjects. Even though these lapses are just a few minutes, they have the capacity to invite chaos. Teachers don't want to just control that possibility; they want to find something that might brighten the day in an important way. When I told several teachers that I was creating a book of short, short stories, arranged in school-month order, that could magically change a mood, teach a lesson, and stimulate imaginations, they only asked, "When will it be finished?"

Where did I find my stories? A few emanated from my own storytelling bag, some resulted from telephone interviews and newspapers, but most came from the public library and my own imagination. As the book grew, so did my idea of its benefits. I realized that by including tales from African, Asian, Hispanic and Native-American folk literature, I could help teachers extend a welcoming hand to students from those cultures. Folk literature works its magic by stimulating the imagination with unusual images. It inspires listeners to feel as one with the reader or teller. It dramatizes age-old concerns and answers questions with which modern generations still struggle. This book is also diverse in its themes. I've included math problem tales, folktales that teach about greed and cleverness, and myths that explain the rainbow, the moon, the sun, and the stars. Who hasn't wondered "Why the Leaves Fall" and "How to Weigh an Elephant?" Folk literature has all the answers, polished with charm and wit.

There's a serious side to folktales, too. When I heard that teachers could use a nonreligious tale that dealt with death, but had an upbeat ending, I included "Ivan and Maryushka." This Russian tale is one that children listen to on one level, but it also speaks to them on a much deeper plane.

As we approach the twenty-first century, it seems our awareness and acceptance of foreign cultures is constantly tested. Television, especially, provokes us to replace our old images with new truths, and it comforts me to find different cultures telling the same folktales. While the tales aren't exactly alike—usually they have different characters and settings—they all share the same themes, teach the same lessons, and ask the same questions. This indicates to me that people all over the world have more in common than we may realize. One story that is an example of this is "Pancakes," a Russian version of "The Cock, the Mouse, and the Little Red Hen." The ancient Jewish tale "Hadrian" can also be recognized as "Fernando and His Neighbor" from Puerto Rico.

When a friend of mine told me about Robby Ferrufino, a brave Hispanic boy battling cancer, I decided to include his story, too. Robby's courage and kindness to the very end of his life is certain to bring tears to your eyes, as it still does to mine. But in a culture like ours that denies death, what a magical moment for a student to become acquainted with the strength of a young boy who dies a hero.

Robby's story was the beginning of adding nonfiction short stories to *Magic Minutes* and to finding new ideas for stories in newspaper articles and telephone interviews. I also looked to science for ideas and found tales about the monarchs, and strange habits of elephants, ostriches, and mosquitoes. I also found stories about kids who accomplished more and had more courage than many adults. "The Boy Who Loved the Woods," and "If You Care, Honk Your Horn" are stories of young heroes and heroines fighting our environmental war. You can't help but be inspired by their youthful daring.

From heroes I went to successful businesses. Wouldn't you like to know how McDonald's got started, or Coca-Cola, or Kentucky Fried Chicken? And of course, I couldn't neglect sports, or the men and women who have been an important part of building our country.

Some children and adults have the ability to consume facts, retain them, and spill them out when needed like a giant computer. However, most of us need a story, or at least an image, to make facts memorable. This is why I included the Indian tales that explain the Spring equinox, March 21, the Fall equinox, September 23, and the Summer and Winter solstices.

During the equinoxes, the sun passes over the equator and everywhere days and nights are of equal length. The Indian story tells us how Spring, robust and fresh, struggles with Ice Man, who does not want to give up his power. At the Fall equinox, the Indians, inadvertently, set fire to a huge poplar tree. Because they fear the spreading fire might burn up the world, they send messengers to the North to convince Ice Man he is needed to bring rain and snow to put out the fire.

Midsummer Eve, or the Summer solstice, celebrates the longest day of the year, about June 22, with a festival memorable for its unusual activities, especially the lighted barrels of dried leaves bouncing down the mountains. My own story, "The Winter Solstice," dramatizes primitive peoples' fear that on the longest night of the year, the sun might not return.

Most of the stories have been retold, some with only slight adaptations, and others with my own style. "The Spring Rains" is a story I wrote to explain the idea of a crybaby bridge, a bit of Oklahoma folklore.

Now that the book is finished, I know it is not just for kids and teachers. It's for libraries, churches, daycare centers, scout leaders, storytellers, and public speakers. It's also a great book for families who still revere a time for stories "between the dark and the daylight" like in Longfellow's "Children's Hour." It might even be one a child could read.

Since this is a book of short, short tales to read aloud, I won't make a long, long introduction. I will only say, I hope the few minutes it takes to read one of my stories will spread a magic over your listeners and yourself that will bring you many minutes of enchantment.

Midsummer Eve, or the Summer solstice, celebrates the longest day of the year, about June 22, with a festival memorable for its unusual activities, especially the lighted barrels of dried leaves bouncing down the mountains. My own story, "The Winter Solstice," dramatizes primitive peoples' fear that on the longest night of the year, the sun might not return.

Most of the stories have been retold, some with only slight adaptations, and others with my own style. "The Spring Rains" is a story I wrote to explain the idea of a crybaby bridge, a bit of Oklahoma folklore.

Now that the book is finished, I know it is not just for kids and teachers. It's for libraries, churches, daycare centers, scout leaders, storytellers, and public speakers. It's also a great book for families who still revere a time for stories "between the dark and the daylight" like in Longfellow's "Children's Hour." It might even be one a child could read.

Since this is a book of short, short tales to read aloud, I won't make a long, long introduction. I will only say, I hope the few minutes it takes to read one of my stories will spread a magic over your listeners and yourself that will bring you many minutes of enchantment.

SEPTEMBER

September

The Corn Fairies' work is over.
No more skipping between the rows,
Singing their songs of hope,
Dancing on their toes.

Now, all is quiet,
The harvest moon's ablaze,
Only the crickets chirp
As Corn Fairies kneel in praise. *

—Pat Nelson

*Inspired by Carl Sandburg's story about Corn Fairies in *Rootabaga Stories*.

1

❦ Have I Got a Fish Story for You! ❧

Did you know there are fish that can walk? Some people even wonder if they can run. In 1960, a fancy fish dealer in Florida imported several 20-inch Asian walking catfish. No one seems to know how they were released from captivity, but it is easy to imagine them marching down the highway on their tails. Actually, walking catfish slither along at a pretty good gait and throw their tales from one side to the other.

Asia has other fish that prefer land, too. The mudskipper hauls itself along the beach on fins tipped with suckers that grip the shore and are capable of gripping the bark of trees. Thailand's catfish don't walk, they waddle on powerful front fins while their tails swing from right to left. They live in the water during the day, but at night they slither out of the water to hunt and migrate. Another fish, the 10-inch freshwater perch, crawls from one flooded rice paddy to another using its fins as legs. It has even been seen climbing trees.

Though these walking fish are plentiful, they have not yet been served to Asian diners. While Asians love fish, they don't like the idea of eating fish that climb trees. They don't like the idea of fish walking down highways either. Luckily, there have been only a few reports of traffic stopped by mudskippers and their friends out for a stroll.

The world has come to know more about these strange fish from an unusual man in Waco, Texas. Braz Walker is an expert on marine life and is particularly interested in walking fish. Braz has written articles and books about walking fish and illustrated the books with his own photography. Remarkably, this Texan has been confined to his bed for 31 years. Braz was stricken with polio at 17 and has been paralyzed from the neck down ever since. His bedroom is filled with mechanical devices that enable him to work. His telephone, cameras, typewriter, and CB radio can all be operated with his tongue. Friends and neighbors also help him.

His bedroom is a busy place all day long. Visitors, especially Waco school children, enjoy hearing Braz tell stories about the fish in the tanks along his walls. Their visits are so pleasing to Braz, that he has added another job. He writes children's stories, not only to educate his young friends about strange life in the sea, but also to capture their imaginations.

❧ The Turtle Who Talked Too Much ❧

Once there was a turtle who talked too much. One day he saw two geese fly in and land on the beach right in front of him.

"Where are you from?" he asked.

The geese answered, "Far, far away where the water is always blue and the trees are always green."

"Wow! That sounds wonderful," Turtle replied. "I wish I could see your home. I know it would be very nice. Is it white? Green? Yellow? Georgian? Early American?" Turtle kept asking and asking questions.

One of the geese interrupted, "Yes, you can! You can come see it. However, you'll not be allowed to talk on the trip. You know, you talk way too much."

Turtle looked a little embarrassed. "Oh, I don't have to talk all the time," he tried to explain. "I know I can stop."

However, he was so excited about the possible trip, he talked and talked and talked. He said he wanted to go, but he didn't have any wings. He thought maybe it was too far to walk. Besides, his legs were too short and his feet hurt. Turtle went on and on and on.

A few days later the geese came to the beach again. This time they were carrying a big, long stick. They told Turtle to grab the stick with his teeth. Then each of the geese grabbed an end of the stick with their bills. They took off with Turtle hanging onto the stick, his teeth clenched as tightly as possible. As they flew over the beach, bathers looked up and pointed at the geese. How they laughed at those geese flying away with a turtle!

But Turtle thought they were laughing at him. He hated being teased. He screamed at them, "Stop laughing! I'm...." Poor Turtle! He never got to explain. When he opened his mouth to talk, he fell down, down, down to the beach and was killed.

As the geese flew back home, one of them said, "I wish Turtle was here. We could have had a great weekend with him."

And the other one answered, "I just feel sad. It's too bad he never learned to keep his mouth shut." [India]

❦ The Duck and the Moon ❧

Once there was a duck swimming along a river looking for fish. The whole day passed without her finding a single one.

When night came she saw the moon reflected on the water and thinking she saw a fish, she dived into the water to catch it. The other ducks saw her, and how they laughed and poked fun at her! The duck was terribly embarrassed.

From that day the duck was so ashamed and so timid that even when she did see a fish underwater, she would not try to catch it. Before long, she died of hunger.

Wasn't she a silly duck for letting herself starve to death rather than learning to laugh at herself? [Leo Tolstoy]

❦ Flying High ❧

One day, arrogant Eagle called all the birds of the world together. "Who can shout as loud as I can?" he asked. Not a bird answered because everyone knew Eagle had the loudest voice in the world. Then Eagle asked, "Who would dare to fight with me?" Again, no one answered. Every bird knew that it couldn't win a fight with Eagle. Finally, Eagle said, "Can any of you fly as high as I can?"

"I can," cried Sparrow in a wee little voice. The other birds were amazed. Sparrow was too tiny to race with Eagle. But the little bird thought someone should try to stop Eagle's overbearing self-importance.

The two birds stood side by side. When Eagle spread his huge wings, everyone admired how big and long and beautiful they were. Just before the big eagle took off, Sparrow hopped onto Eagle's back. Sparrow was so little that Eagle took off unaware of him. When Eagle was far above the mountain peaks, he wondered where Sparrow was. "Sparrow? Sparrow? Where are you?" he called.

"Here," said Sparrow in his wee little voice from above Eagle's head. How strange, thought Eagle. That Sparrow is just above my head. Eagle flew higher and called again. Sparrow answered as before, still sitting on Eagle's back. Eagle became angry because he knew Sparrow was above him. He was afraid that little bird was going to win. Driven by fear, Eagle tried to fly higher, but it was too much for him. His wings went limp and he fell to the ground. When Sparrow realized what was happening, he took off from Eagle and flew back to his bird friends who believed he was a hero. [Indonesia]

❧ The Little Man Who Wanted ❧ to Grow Tall

Once upon a time, there was a very little man who had a great longing to grow taller. He wanted to grow as tall as a tree. Year after year went by and he didn't grow at all, so he decided to ask the horse for advice.

When the little man found the horse he said, "Would you tell me, horse, what I should do to become as big as you?"

The horse looked the man over and said, "Well, I think that if you eat plenty of oats and straw and get plenty of exercise by running around the field, in a few weeks' time you should be as big as me."

The little man went back home and did just as the horse suggested, but he didn't grow an inch. All he got was indigestion from eating straw and pains in his legs from running. He decided that the horse didn't know anything, but maybe the bull would be a bit smarter.

When the little man asked the bull how to become bigger, the bull tossed his head and said, "Eat lots of grass and hay and spend all day lying down chewing the cud. If you do that you'll soon be as big as I am."

The little man returned home and he did everything the bull had advised. He ate plenty of grass and hay and chewed the cud, but he didn't grow. All he got was indigestion from the grass and hay and a backache from lying around all day.

The little man decided to ask the owl for advice. The owl was supposed to be the wisest creature in the forest. When the little man found the owl, he said, "Owl, you have to help me grow taller. I want to be as tall as a tree."

The owl said, "What on earth for?"

"I want to be able to see long distances. All I ever see are knees and weeds."

The owl closed his eyes wearily. "Why don't you climb a tree?" he murmured.

"Oh, I didn't think of that!" the little man answered, his face flushed with embarrassment.

The owl opened his eyes and looked the little man square in the face. "Take it from me," he said. "If a man has a brain and uses it, it doesn't matter what size he is. He's big enough for anything." [Africa]

❧ The Boy Who Loved the Woods ❧

Andrew Holleman was similar to many other boys because he loved sports. Swimming was a favorite, but he liked team sports, too, such as soccer. When he wasn't participating in sports, he had his nose in a book or he was involved in his hobby, an activity that not only gave him great enjoyment, but ultimately recognition.

Andrew's playground was a 17-acre plot of soggy, second-growth forest in Chelmsford, Massachusetts. He spent hours there every day identifying small animals, birds, and wildflowers. Through his study, Andrew learned much about pollution and ground water.

One day it was announced that an $11 million, 180-unit complex was proposed for the site of Andrew's playground. When he heard the news, he forgot his usual shyness. All he could think about was fighting the construction. "No way they're going to build those condos here," Andrew yelled at anyone who would listen.

A neighbor responded, "You can't fight City Hall, Andrew."

"But I've got to do something," Andrew replied, sounding rather desperate. "This development will kill the wildlife and pollute the water. That land is just too wet for building."

Andrew became busy writing letters to everyone he knew, to his legislators, and even to the Boston TV anchors. Finally, he called the Audubon Society for advice. The woman on the other end of the line listened patiently. When Andrew finished, she said, "Go to town council meetings and speak your mind. Tell your neighbors. Get everyone mad about it."

At that moment, Andrew was certain he was in over his head. He felt so alone as he told the lady on the phone that he was only 12 years old. But she didn't care how old he was! She knew Andrew was well-informed and could get the job done. In her most business-like manner, she kindly told him to get busy.

Andrew was a little shocked, but he did everything the Audubon Society suggested. Each job gave him more courage. Finally, in the Spring of 1988, "deep-hole" soil and ground water tests were done. The tests were just as he had predicted. His wonderful playground flunked! The land couldn't absorb any more water. It was a great day for Andrew!

Andrew is again enjoying his wonderful hobby. He had his playground again, plus a community service award from his principal and awards from the U.S. Environmental Protection Agency and the United Nations Environmental Programme.

Everyone in Chelmsford thinks Andrew is a pretty great kid.

⦃ Chi and Yi ⦄

Chi and Yi had just become friends. They enjoyed many things together, especially walking in the woods.

One day, Chi, who was the larger boy, saw a bear coming their way in the woods. Quickly, he climbed a tree but he didn't tell his friend about the approaching danger. When Yi finally saw the bear, he didn't have time to climb the tree, so he quickly fell to the ground and pretended he was dead.

The bear, curious, went over to Yi. He licked the boy with his tongue and then sniffed a long time at Yi's ear. Finally, the bear went on his way and Yi stood up.

Chi, still up on a high limb in the tree, called out, "What did that bear whisper in your ear, Yi?"

Yi answered, "He told me he had already eaten his dinner and wasn't hungry. Then he suggested that after this, I choose friends who don't think only of themselves." [China]

⦃ The Wise Cook ⦄

There once was a king who loved to eat. When the castle cook grew too old to prepare his meals anymore, the king looked for a new cook. A young man applied for the job. The king said to him, "I want you to cook me the best and most important dish in the whole world."

That night the king sat down at the table. When he looked at the special dish, he said, "Why, that's cow tongue!"

The young man answered, "Yes, it is. Nothing is more important than the tongue if it is used correctly. The tongue is used to teach, to explain, to command, to defend, to calm. Tongues are used to sing to babies and to make bargains. Tongue has to be the most important thing for a king."

"I must say I didn't realize that, young man. You've opened my eyes. Therefore, tomorrow night, I want you to fix me the worst dish you know."

The next night, the young man served the king cow tongue. The king said, "What goes on here? Last night, tongue was the best dish in the world. Tonight it is the worst? How could this be?"

"The difference is what you do with it," said the young man. "Tongues make gossip, stir up trouble, and tell lies. Tongues are cruel and hypocritical. Therefore, tongue can be the worst dish in the world."

"Yes, I see. I also see that I need your wisdom in my court. I'll get someone else to do the cooking." [Africa]

❦ Sequoyah ❧

Sequoyah was a Cherokee Indian who dreamed of bringing a special gift to his people. Because of Sequoyah, many Cherokee tales have been preserved.

The Cherokees say that books are white man's magic and call them "talking leaves." Sequoyah wanted his people to have their own books. Because no Cherokee alphabet existed, Sequoyah decided to create one. He started by making a character for each word. But there were too many words. Then it occurred to him that words were really sounds. If he could just capture all the sounds and make characters for them, he would have an alphabet, he thought.

Sequoyah became so enthusiastic about his idea that he spent all of his time following his people so he could listen to their speech. He made such a nuisance of himself—interrupting and asking everyone to repeat what they had just said—that the Cherokees wished he would go away. Even his wife was angry with him.

The work took many years. When it was finished, he showed his tribe not an alphabet, but a syllabary* of 86 characters that represented syllables or sounds easily learned in two days. The Cherokees, quickly forgetting their many years of irritation with Sequoyah, wanted to know when they could get their own "talking leaves."

Sequoyah spent most of his life either dreaming about or creating a written language for his people. Now that it was completed, he spent his time teaching the Cherokee children to read, who in turn taught their parents. The tribe printed a Cherokee bible, newspaper, and established Cherokee schools. The Cherokees were filled with pride when they realized the unique contribution of Sequoyah's gift. Today, they would learn that Sequoyah was the first person in the history of the world to create an alphabet or a syllabary all by himself.

The United States has honored him, too. In Statuary Hall in Washington, D.C., only one statue stands of an American Indian, and that Indian is Sequoyah. California honored him by naming the state's great redwood trees Sequoias. A mountain on the Tennessee and North Carolina border also was given his name.

Sequoyah was a simple man who achieved greatness because he dedicated his time and energy to a dream that had great purpose. [Cherokee Indian]

---

* syllabary: a series or set of written characters, each one of which is used to represent a syllable

❦ Reading Isn't Easy ❦

It was the first day of school, and Beverly was miserable. Her mother had just settled her in her seat in the classroom and was now at the door looking her way. Beverly offered a half-hearted wave. She didn't understand why her mother said they had to move to town now that she was entering first grade. She wished she was back on the farm.

Out of the corner of her eye Beverly saw the boy across the aisle scoop up a finger full of white paste, put it in his mouth, and swallow it. Beverly's eyes glazed and she thought she was going to throw up. She turned back to the front and looked at a painting of a pretty little girl in a white party dress above the blackboard to make herself feel better. Beverly wished she was wearing a white party dress, instead of the blue serge one she had on that scratched her every place it touched.

The teacher called the class to order and passed out some readers with olive green covers and big black print. Expectantly, Beverly opened the cover of her reader, scowled, and hastily thumbed through to the end. Where were the pictures? All books for children have pictures—at least the ones in her mother's library in the village near their farm did.

Beverly was very disappointed with school. However, she did want to learn to read, and she was certain it would be easy. But day after day went by and Beverly did not learn.

One morning, her teacher said, "There will be three reading groups: Bluebirds, Redbirds, and Blackbirds." Beverly, a Blackbird, was with all the boys who fooled around during class. Most of the girls were Bluebirds. She saw one Bluebird whispering to the girl in front of her, and then they both pointed at Beverly and giggled. Beverly felt disgraced!

She didn't learn to read that first year or even the second. But with the third year came success. It was as though someone pulled up a shade inside Beverly's head and the magic of sunshine made it possible for her to read. She read everything: books, signs, letters, cans, boxes, even headlines. Every word she saw she tried to read. And then Beverly began writing stories. When she grew up she wrote books. A few of those books are *Ramona the Brave*, *Ramona and Her Father*, *Ramona and Her Mother*, *Ramona Quimby Age 8*, *Ralph S. Mouse*, *Dear Mr. Henshaw*, and *Ramona Forever*. Of course, that little girl who couldn't read was Beverly Cleary.

⚓ The Man Who Liked Money ⚓ Better Than Life

In Shanghai there were many good swimmers. One day, the river suddenly swelled. In spite of the dangerous water level a small group of people decided to cross the river in a small boat. While still in midstream, the boat capsized. Everyone began swimming for the river bank. One, however, though he used his arms vigorously, seemed to make little progress across the river.

His friends called to him. "Hurry up! You're a better swimmer than any of us. Why are you lagging behind?"

The man gasped, "I have a thousand coins tied around my waist."

"Why don't you throw them away?" his friends called. "We're afraid you might drown and none of us is good enough to save you."

The man made no answer, but just shook his head as though he was clearly in great difficulty.

When the others reached the shore and saw the man had made little progress, they shouted, "Untie the coin belt! Let it go, you fool! The money is no good to you if you drown."

Still the man shook his head, and within a few minutes, he drowned. [China]

⚓ The Houseboat Mystery ⚓

Have you ever dreamed of living on a houseboat? Instead of going to the grocery store, you could dangle a fish hook in the water. Quite a few American children do live on houseboats. They say that sometimes it's fun, but sometimes it is very strange.

In San Francisco in 1985, the people who lived in Richardson Bay on houseboats complained about a humming noise in the night. It became so loud that they couldn't sleep. At first they guessed it came from underground electrical power lines or a diesel generator. Finally, they concluded it didn't come from the land at all. It was an underwater sound. So the residents brought in some acoustical* engineers from Berkeley to locate the sound.

What was keeping everyone awake? A fish! A singing toadfish! "Little Ugly" was the name the kids gave this crazy fish because he was fat and thick with a flat head. The male toadfish sings love songs to his mate. If he thinks there are any other male toadfish hanging around her, he makes sure they hear his song as a warning to stay away.

"Little Ugly" isn't the only strange fish. There's also an oyster toadfish that whistles. The electric catfish hisses. The horse mackerel grunts like a pig. Trunk-fishes and puffers sound just like growling dogs, and the family of fish called drums can creak, hum, purr, and whistle.

Still think you'd like to live on a houseboat?

---

* acoustical: relating to sounds or to the science of sounds

⚛ The Endless Tale ⚛

In the Far East there was a great king who had no work to do. Every day and all day long he sat on his soft cushions and listened to stories. It didn't matter what the stories were about, he never grew tired of hearing them, even though they could be very long.

"There is only one fault that I find with your story," he often said to a storyteller. "It is too short!"

All of the storytellers in the world had been invited to his palace, and some told tales that were very long. But the King was always sad when the story ended.

One day the King announced that anyone who could tell him a tale that would never end would receive a prize. "I will give my fairest daughter to be the winner's wife and he will inherit the throne after me." The King also said that any man who tried and failed would be beheaded.

Many young men tried but didn't accomplish the task. However, one day a handsome stranger from the south arrived at the palace and asked if he might try. The King sat down and the storyteller began: "Once upon a time a certain king seized all the corn in his country and stored it away in a strong granary. But a swarm of locusts came over the land and saw where the grain had been put. After searching for many days, the swarm found a crevice on the east side of the granary that was just large enough for one locust to pass through at a time. So one locust went in and carried out a grain of corn. Then another locust went in and carried out a grain of corn. Then another locust went in and carried out a grain of corn."

Day after day, week after week, the storyteller continued "Then another locust went in and carried out a grain of corn."

A month passed; a year passed. At the end of two years the King said, "How much longer will the locusts be going in and carrying out the corn?"

"O, King!" said the storyteller. "They have as yet cleared only one cubit*" and there are many thousand cubits in the granary."

Suddenly, the King's face turned red and he screamed, "Man, man! You will drive me mad. I can listen to your story no longer. Take my daughter and be my heir, but do not let me hear another word about those horrible locusts!"

And so the King's daughter and the storyteller were married and lived happily in the land for many years. The King lived for a long time and never once asked the storyteller to tell him a story because he was so afraid he would be told an endless tale. [Canada]

---

* cubit: an ancient term for the distance between the elbow and the tip of the middle finger, about 18 to 21 inches

⟨ The Sun Gazer ⟩

Once there was an Indian boy who early in life deeply loved the sun. Just before dawn each morning he would climb a hill outside his tepee village. There he would sit and watch the bright sun on its journey across the sky. Sometimes he would sing songs in praise of the sun, but he never took his eyes away from its brilliance. Because of this love, the boy was named Sun Gazer.

The elders of the tribe warned Sun Gazer about the dangers of his great love. "If you continue to stare at the sun," the chief said, "you will become blind." Sun Gazer listened respectfully to the chief's words, but continued to stare at the sun. And one day Sun Gazer became blind.

But even blindness didn't stop him. He continued to climb the hill early each morning. Guided by the heat of the sun's rays on his face, Sun Gazer followed the sun on its daily course. But in the darkness of blindness, he lost interest in life. He didn't talk to his friends or his family. Eventually, he didn't eat. He grew weaker and weaker and was often sad.

One evening after sundown, when Sun Gazer did not return from his favorite place on the hill, a search party was sent out. They found him facing west. The last spark of life had left him as the final rays of the sun disappeared.

The tribe buried Sun Gazer on the very top of that hill. The next morning when they returned to visit the grave, they saw that a tall, graceful flower had sprung from the mound and was gently nodding in the breeze. As they watched, they found that it, too, turned its face toward the sun as the sun made its journey across the sky.

The flower has come to be known as the sunflower. If you watch one, you will notice that no matter where the sun is in the sky, the sunflower's face is always turned toward it. [Native American]

❧ The Tree That Wouldn't ❧ Stop Burning

One morning in Fall several boys who lived in a tepee village decided to burn the weeds and tall grass that covered their ball field. When the fire became uncontrollable the boys ran to their fathers for help.

The fathers quickly put out the fire, but the branches of an old poplar tree still burned. They worked hard all day long to extinguish the fire and still the tree burned. Finally, the entire top of the tree fell to the ground. After the boys stamped out all of the sparks, the boys and their fathers cheered. At last, the fire was out!

The next morning they were surprised to see the tree still burning. Upon investigation, the fire was discovered to have gone down into the tree's roots and was burning a huge hole in the ground. Everyone threw water on the fire, but the flames would not subside. The men and boys became frightened and wondered if the whole world would burn.

The chief called a council meeting. The tribe's wisest men sat in a circle in the council house to study the problem. Finally, an elderly Indian said, "There is a man in the north who can put out this fire. His name is Ice Man. We need to send him a message." The younger men laughed at such an idea. But the chief knew it was a good plan and chose two of his best runners to carry the message. The rest of the tribe kept watch over the fire while they were gone.

After many days of running, the messengers found Ice Man. He was a small man with white braids that hung to the ground. He quickly assured them he could help and began unbraiding his hair.

When it was hanging loose, he grabbed his hair in his hand and hit his other hand with it. The young men felt a cold wind blow on their faces. Then Ice Man struck his palm with his hair until rain began to fall softly. He struck his palm again and the rain turned into sleet. He struck one more time and hailstones fell all around them.

Ice Man said to the messengers, "Go back now to your people and tell them what you have seen. I will arrive after you are home."

When they returned, the messengers found their people sadly watching smoke rise from deep cracks in the earth. The next day there was a cold wind, but it only made the fire blaze. When a light rain fell, it seemed to make the fire hotter. Finally, sleet and hail worked together to put out the fire. Steam and dark smoke filled the air as the village people ran to their homes. While they slept that night, a strong wind blew rain and hail deep into the roots of the old poplar tree until there was nothing left to burn.

The next day revealed no smoke, only rain. It rained for so many days that the people complained to the Great Spirit, "Ice Man is playing a trick on us. We are tired of not seeing the sun."

They say that the Great Spirit sent Ice Man back to the north, but not before the Great Spirit had a little laugh with him about Ice Man's trick. [Native American]

❧ Wunderkinder ❧

Wunderkinder, or wonder children, was the name given by the German people to describe the many brilliant children born in Germany during the early 18th century. Some of these children learned to speak at 10 months of age, and by the age of three these children were fluent in several languages. Some were geniuses at math and law, and some were musicians. One of these musicians, Wolfgang Amadeus Mozart, became one of the greatest composers of music the world has ever known.

Born in 1756, Wolfgang was only three years old when his father, Leopold, discovered him playing the piano. Wolfgang had learned by watching his sister, Nannerl, who was a very talented pianist. When Wolfgang was four years old and beginning to compose little songs, his father knew his son was a genius. Leopold immediately began planning a lengthy tour of Europe to show off his children to the world.

At seven years old, Wolfgang was ready for the tour. By that time he could play the clavier* with a cloth covering the keyboard, as well as with the keys visible to him. He also played the violin and spent many hours composing each day. Wolfgang could compose a complete sonata** in his mind without writing it down until much later. Wolfgang's perfect pitch enabled him to name a note played without error. Is it any wonder that when Leopold finally took his children on that long awaited tour, European audiences were wild with delight. The Mozart children were showered with money and jewels and were treated the same way we treat rock stars today.

Though Mozart's life was short, only 35 years, every day was lived for music. He composed more than 600 pieces, including operas, symphonies, masses, and religious music.

The brilliance of Mozart's music is because it is as fresh and full of life today as the day it was written. But that is to be expected of "wunderkinder."

---

*   clavier: an early keyboard instrument

** sonata: instrumental musical composition

OCTOBER

October Wind

She dances down the mountain
Crying the song of the gypsy fiddle.
Gray chiffon whirling,
Twirling,
And swirling.
Barefoot, she pirouettes
Into the bonfire
While black embers glow
Like ripe persimmons,
And singed leaves flutter
Into the sky.
Breathless, she pauses,
Poses like a gazelle
Trembling with expectation.
Suddenly, she leaps from
Tree to bush
Back up the mountain,
Spreading the gossip
Of approaching Winter.

—Pat Nelson

❧ Why the Leaves Fall ❧

Many moons ago when the world was still very young, the plants and animals were enjoying the beautiful Summer weather. But as time went by, Autumn set in, and the weather became colder with each passing day.

The grasses and flowers were in a sad condition, for they had no protection from the bitter cold. Just when it seemed that there was no hope for living, the Great Spirit came to their aid. He said the leaves of the trees should fall to the ground, spreading a soft, warm blanket over the tender roots of the grasses and flowers. To repay the trees for the loss of their leaves, the Great Spirit gave them one last bright array of beauty.

That is why, each year during Indian Summer, the trees take on their beautiful farewell colors of red, gold, and brown. After this final display, they turn to their appointed task, covering the earth with a thick rug of warmth against the chill of Winter. [Native American]

❧ How the Ducks Got Their Colors ❧

A young warrior, who since childhood had been very fond of bright colors, once walked far away from camp. He loved the beautiful colors of Indian Summer. Now and then he would stop and take from his pouch some clay and oil to paint the colors he saw. As the shadows grew long, he knew it would soon be time for the night fire, so he made his way to a nearby lake where he built his camp.

As he sat looking at the red sun that was about to set under the colored sky, he heard the talk of waterfowl coming toward him. He saw large and small ducks, gray geese, and loons diving and playing. They were all his friends and he was glad to see them. He cupped his hands around his mouth and called to them. They were startled at first, but when they recognized him they paddled to shore.

The ducks and the young man enjoyed each other's company. When the young warrior told them he had been studying and mixing colors, a gray duck became interested. "Since you are our friend," said the duck, "would you be so kind as to paint us with your beautiful colors?"

"I will," said the warrior. "Just choose your colors."

The large gray duck decided that he wished a pretty green head with a white stripe around his neck, a brown breast, and yellow legs. We call these mallard ducks.

The mallard flapped his wings and said, "Please don't paint my mate the same colors." So the warrior painted her mostly brown.

Then the teal duck had himself and his family painted as he desired. The warrior used all his greens and blues and cinnamon colors on them. With his paints gone, the warrior couldn't paint the goose and the loon. To this day, the goose and the loon remain dull gray. [Native American]

❦ The Sun Never Sets on Kitty ❧

The 19th century British Biologist, Thomas H. Huxley, (grandfather of Brave New World author, Aldous Huxley) once explained, only half in jest, why the British empire owed its power to the love of elderly spinsters for pet cats. His argument resembled one used in all seriousness by Charles Darwin, a founder of the theory of evolution, and it illustrates the complex links between different forms of life. It went like this:

Because spinsters liked cats, they often kept them as pets. The cats kept down the numbers of field mice, thus reducing the mice's raids on the nests of bees, the only insects that pollinate red clover. As a result, red clover grew abundantly in the pastures around farming villages and provided British cattle with a nutritious diet. The plentiful supply of high quality beef kept British sailors strong and healthy, thus improving the fighting quality of the Royal Navy, which guarded and extended the British empire around the world.

❧ Big Ghost, Little Ghost ❧

Charlie was 6 and his brother, Martin, was 12 when they moved to a farm. Martin loved the farm, but Charlie was too scared to enjoy it. He was afraid of the cow, the pig, the chickens, and the dark, scary, dirt path that wound through the dark woods to the mailbox.

Charlie's mother gave him little sympathy. "I know you're only six," she said, "but you're not too young to fight fear. The next time you are scared, stand still and really look at what is scaring you. Then tell yourself to be brave. You'll find out there is not much around here that could hurt you."

Charlie tried it. He discovered cow's swishing tail couldn't hurt him, and pig was just noisy. He ran toward the chickens and they scurried away. But the dirt path was more difficult. Several weeks passed before Charlie conquered his fear of the dirt path winding through the dark woods.

Just before Halloween Charlie's parents gave him a pet monkey to show how proud they felt about the way he was growing up. Charlie named him Toto and they became good friends.

The night before Halloween Charlie started down the dirt path to the mailbox. Martin saw him and had an idea, but he needed a costume. He found an old sheet, cut two holes in it for eyes, and threw it over his head. Martin planned to wait by the gate to the dirt path, and when Charlie came around that last bend, Martin intended to scare him.

Martin didn't know that Toto, being a monkey, just had to copy him. When he saw Martin dressed in a sheet, Toto found a big, white towel, put it over his head like a scarf and held it together under his chin with one hand.

As Charlie came around the bend, he gasped when he saw the big ghost at the gate and jumped behind a tree right into some prickly weeds. When he was brave enough, he peeked around the tree trunk and shivered when he realized the ghost was waiting for him. And then he saw Toto run up behind Martin and pull off his sheet. Martin let out the most frightened yell Charlie had ever heard and ran as fast as he could up the walk towards the house with Toto after him.

Suddenly, Charlie thought Martin looked so funny running away from little Toto that he called, "Hey, big ghost, are you afraid of a little ghost?"

It was the greatest Halloween Charlie ever had. [Pat Nelson]

❧ A Ghost at the Door ❧

One night in a little village where danger seldom lurked, a young couple was awakened by a pounding on their door. Because it was so late and they expected no one, they were too frightened to get out of bed. The pounding continued, but they put their pillows over their heads and finally went back to sleep.

They awakened in the morning to a house in disarray. Furniture was tipped over. Drawers were emptied and feathers from torn pillows covered everything. The couple spent the day cleaning up the mess and talking to the neighbors about their misfortune.

That night there was pounding again. This time the man called from his bed, "Who are you?" There was no answer, so he called again, "Who are you?"

The voice on the other side of the door let out a painful cry, and then another. There was a pause, and then a sad, shaky voice said, "Why did you take my shoes? I need them. Give them back."

Tears filled the couples' eyes when they recognized their grandfather's voice. They had buried him the week before and had kept his shoes for themselves. They didn't think he'd be needing them in a grave.

Finally, the man called to his grandfather, "Grandad, you go back to the grave. We will bring your shoes in the morning." And the old man did.

The next morning, when the sky was barely pink, the couple hurried to the cemetery and put the shoes on top of their grandfather's grave. After that, he rested in peace. [Lithuania]

❧ Big Pumpkin and Big Kettle ❧

Farmer Bill always bragged about his crop of big pumpkins. "One of my pumpkins was so big I couldn't load it on the wagon. I had to leave it in the field all winter," he said. In the Spring, he found the sow he had missed in December living inside that pumpkin with her 10 new babies.

Farmer Bill's neighbor became sick and tired of his pumpkin tales. One day the neighbor decided he was going to tell Farmer Bill a taller tale than he had ever thought of telling.

The next time he visited Farmer Bill, the neighbor said, "On that trip I took last week, I visited a factory that was making a kettle 100 feet across."

Farmer Bill asked, "What would anyone want with a kettle that big?"

His neighbor replied, "They were making that kettle just to cook that big pumpkin of yours." [American Tall Tale]

⟨ Success ⟩

Maurice and Dick were brothers who dreamed of success. They wanted to be movie stars so much that they left their home in New Hampshire in the 1920s and hurried to Hollywood.

The brothers soon discovered that becoming movie stars wasn't very easy. They didn't have any luck at all. They were tempted to return home and forget about their dreams, but they didn't. Instead, Maurice and Dick got jobs managing a theater. If they couldn't be stars themselves, they could at least watch screen stars every day while they worked.

They'd been working just a few months when the Depression hit. Industries shut down. People lost their jobs. No one had enough money to go to the movies. Their theater careers came to a quick end, and once again they looked for work.

Maurice and Dick tried other small businesses, but it always ended the same way. No one could make a business go during the Depression. These were hard times, but somehow they never lost their courage.

In 1937, they borrowed some money and opened a drive-in restaurant in Pasadena, California. Maurice and Dick were an instant success. When they opened a second restaurant and it was a winner, too, they dreamed of a chain of restaurants. They wanted a restaurant that could provide good food quickly. They shortened their menu: HAMBURGERS—15¢...FRENCH FRIES—15¢. They streamlined their kitchen and changed from a drive-in to a regular restaurant specializing in fast food. Their advertising motto became SIMPLE...GOOD FOOD...FAST! It was exactly what the people wanted— good, plain food in a hurry.

Dick and Maurice were cautious businessmen who thought carefully before making changes. One day they agreed to add milkshakes to their menu. Within one week, Mr. Ray Kroc was in their office taking an order for eight multi-mixers. He came all the way from Chicago to take the order himself so he could see what kind of a restaurant would want to make 48 milkshakes at once.

Ray Kroc liked what he saw and asked the McDonald brothers for the opportunity to buy a franchise. Reluctantly, they sold him one and soon he wanted another. In 1961 the brothers sold Ray Kroc their interest, including secret formulas, trademarks, and franchises for more than $2.5 million. Neither Dick nor Maurice lived to see McDonald's become the multinational corporation it is today.

A Clever Judge

Long ago in China, a man complained that someone had stolen his pearl-handled knife. The police tried to find the thief, but all they came up with were suspects. A judge who was known for his cleverness was called in. After hearing from accused and accuser, the judge said, "I know of a temple whose bell can tell a thief from an honest man. It has great spiritual powers."

The bell was brought to court. It was shrouded in a black curtain. The suspects were told they would each have to touch the bell. If they were guilty, the bell would ring.

Secretly, the judge had one of his assistants slip behind the black curtain and paint the bell with black ink.

As the judge led each suspect to the bell to touch it, the room remained silent, and there was no sound from the bell. After the last suspect had touched the bell, the judge asked all suspects to hold their hands in front of them with palms up. All were smudged with black ink except one. He had been afraid to touch the bell for fear it would ring. He was the thief. [China]

The Man and His Two Wives

Back in the old days, when it was all right for a man to have two wives at the same time, there was a man who had an old wife and a young wife. He soon learned to be very careful with them so they wouldn't fight.

One day, the old wife was combing the man's hair. She had gray hair, and she wanted her husband to look her age. So each time she found a black hair, she pulled it out. The man yelled, "Ow!"

The young wife said, "Here, let me comb your hair. She just pulled out some of your beautiful black hairs," and she grabbed the comb from the old wife.

As the young woman combed the man's hair, every time she saw a gray hair, she pulled it out. Soon, the man was about to cry. He said, "Please, leave me alone. I'll comb my own hair." But the two wives did not stop.

What happened? The man became as bald as a billiard ball. [East India]

How Frog Lost His Tail

When you think about it, Frog really is a pretty ugly animal—eyes like head-lights, lumpy skin, and a mouth so big that if you looked inside, you would see all the way down to his tail. That is, if he had a tail, which he doesn't.

It was the tail that bothered Frog the most. It bothered him so much he decided to ask Sky God for a tail. "What do you need it for?" Sky God asked.

"I look so awful," Frog answered, and almost cried.

"Oh, stop that crybaby stuff. I'll tell you what I'll do. I'll make a deal. You can have a tail if you'll be a watchman for a special well that doesn't dry up."

Frog agreed and his tail was beautiful. He loved it so much that he became conceited. He yelled and hollered at all the animals. And when the other wells dried up, he would scream at the animals at his well, "Go away! Go away! The well is dry."

Frog was so rude that Sky God heard about it and paid a visit to the well, in disguise of course. When Frog treated Sky God like he treated the other animals, Sky God was furious. He took away Frog's tail and sent him away from the well.

Now, the only time Frog has a tail is when he is a tadpole. He still complains about it, but it does no good. He just can't handle a beautiful tail. [Africa]

⚜ How to Tell a Spooky Story ⚜

Just because you have learned a spooky story to tell doesn't mean you are automatically going to frighten people into screaming. There are a few little tricks to make people shiver and shake.

First, never say, "Do you want to hear a spooky story?"

What's wrong with that? Already you've told them you want to scare them. That won't work because people generally aren't scared unless they're startled or surprised. So remember, with your most peaceful, gentle face say, "Hi! I thought you might like to hear a story I just learned."

Then tell your story slowly in a whispery voice. It's good if your listeners have to concentrate on hearing you. In the story, *Dark Night*, when you come to the next to the last line, drag out the last two words so they think the story is over. As soon as you let go of the word "door," scream as loud as you can, "I saw a ghost!"

Dark Night

On a dark, dark night
Near a dark, dark road
I saw a dark, dark house
With a long, dark porch.
I opened the dark, dark door
And went into a dark, dark bedroom
I saw a dark, dark closet.
When I opened the dark, dark door
I SAW A GHOST!

❧ The Monarch ❧

The beauty of the monarch butterfly almost takes your breath away. Its huge wings—orange as the sun and outlined in black and white—are dazzling. Every year millions of these butterflies escape Winter cold by sailing across the sky to the Sierra Madre in Mexico.

Usually monarchs lead a lonesome life. But when that first breeze whispers "Winter," they band together in huge swarms and fly as far as 2,000 miles to their Mexican haven. Actually, they don't really fly, nor do they flutter. They flap their wings once or twice and then coast on the wind. Scientists think they either navigate by the sun or follow landmarks, such as mountains or rivers. But most groups of monarchs fly from northeast to southwest across the United States and then to the Yucatan Peninsula.

Monarchs only live for about six weeks, just long enough for the birth of three to four generations. When it is time to glide north again, only grand-children and great-grandchildren are alive to make the trip. There's no one to tell them where to go, and yet they all go back to where their ancestors came from.

Watch for the monarchs in the Fall. They usually begin travelling in August and swarm in trees along the way. While resting, they dress the tree in orange, white, and black, completely disguising its identity. If they ever choose to rest in a tree in your yard, watch for them the following year. They very often use that resting place again.

A Feathery Puzzle

What kind of bird eats grass, leaves, fruit, stones, pebbles, watches, metal, jewelry, and even bits of glass, and can kick hard enough to break a human leg?

Give up? The answer is an ostrich. The bird typically weighs 300 pounds and is 8 feet tall. It has only two tiny toes on each of its two long legs, which makes it difficult for the ostrich to balance its large body, long neck, and small, flat head. It can't fly because its wings aren't strong enough to carry it through the air.

An ostrich is capable of running 30 miles per hour using 14-foot steps. It can easily outrun its enemies. In the past it was believed that the ostrich hid from its enemies by burying its head in the sand. This is no longer considered true. However, this bird sometimes for some unknown reason chooses to run around and around in a circle, which makes it easy prey.

Today, most ostriches are raised in Africa for their meat, feathers, and hide. In the United States, curious Americans pay to view them on private, wild animal farms, and owners sell their plumes and eggshells to artistic craftsmen. The Scott Smith family, from Fairfield, Iowa, toured one of these farms in the family's open jeep. The driver brought food for the animals. The Smiths fed the llamas and zebras with no trouble. However, as they approached the ostriches, the driver yelled, "Get down!" One of the ostriches was running down the road after them! When the ostrich caught up with the jeep, it continued running alongside. Occasionally, it would try to bite someone though the family was huddled on the floor for protection. The Smiths' heavy clothing protected them, but needless to say, they probably are not interested in an ostrich for a pet!

❦ The Haunted House ❧

In a little town there was an old grandfather who lived in a haunted house. A boy who had just moved to town laughed at the idea that the old man's house was haunted. One time when the old man was going on a little trip, he invited the kid to house-sit for him. The boy jumped at the chance, thinking he'd show this town how brave he was.

He packed a lunch for himself. Because he had seen some loose boards in the floor, he brought his carpenter's apron and some tools. He liked working with wood and he was pretty good for someone so young. He thought he'd help the old man out a bit. After he had worked several hours, he said, "Huh, just as I thought. There's not a spook in the place. Guess it's time to have some supper."

After supper, he decided to read. He was deep into his story when he heard, "Whoooo ooooo!" He jumped out of the chair and ran over to the fireplace. It sounded as if the noise was coming from the chimney. However, he only received soot in his face for his trouble, so he went back to reading. In the middle of a story, he heard a door creak. He jumped again. Like a madman, he ran all through the house, opening and looking behind all the doors, but he didn't find a thing. He realized he was pretty scared and decided the best thing to do was to pick up his tools and get to work. He put on his apron, knelt down on the floor, and started pounding. He worked fast and nervously. As he was nailing down the boards, he accidently nailed his apron to the floor. When he couldn't get up, he thought a ghost had nailed him down. He became so scared he fainted, and the town had a good laugh. [Ireland]

❧ Teddy ❧

Some children, almost from the day they are born, have trouble breathing. Teddy Roosevelt was one of them. Many a night his father bundled him up and took him for a ride in their carriage up and down the empty New York City streets. He hoped the gentle ocean breeze would bring his son relief. Sometimes it did, and sometimes it didn't. But in spite of having asthma, Teddy had a wonderful childhood and went on to have a full and exciting life.

Teddy and his two cousins were inseparable as children. They collected bones, stones, dead mice, birds, frogs, and anything else they thought was interesting. Teddy especially loved to collect toads and often carried them on his head under his hat. They kept accurate records of their collection in their diaries and hid it all in a dresser drawer until they could realize their dream of opening the Roosevelt Museum of Natural History.

Teddy was a happy boy, even though he was sickly. When he became older, his father put a gymnasium in their home. He hoped Teddy would work to build up his body. But Teddy wasn't interested in the gym until he was bullied by two young men and wasn't strong enough to fight back. After that, he took boxing lessons and worked out every day to build his strength. His hard work paid off when Teddy entered college and became a member of Harvard University's boxing team.

Teddy (whose given name was Theodore) became a man of tremendous energy and spirit. He led the Rough Riders (soldiers on horseback) in the Spanish-American War. Then the president appointed him secretary of the navy. Next he became vice-president of the United States. When President William McKinley was assassinated, Teddy Roosevelt became our 26th president.

He still spent as much time as possible outdoors, especially hunting big game. It was on one of these hunting trips that he had an unusual experience with a bear cub. Roosevelt and his friends were standing in a small clearing, waiting for someone to spot some game. Suddenly, from behind a bush came a young bear cub. It stopped right in front of the president. His friends hollered, "Shoot him!" But to Roosevelt that would have been like shooting a child. The cub was too young and innocent, and he refused.

Clifford K. Berryman, cartoonist for the *Washington Star*, heard the story and drew a cartoon of Roosevelt saving the life of the bear cub. He called the cub "Teddy Bear." "Teddy Bear" was picked up by toymakers. At first they created stuffed bears that looked like Roosevelt. Eventually, that changed and teddy bear became the name given to all stuffed bears.

Theodore Roosevelt was born October 27, 1858. It's fun to remember that because of him, we have teddy bears. However, let's also remember that because he loved the outdoors so much, he fought for and established our national public park system.

❦ The Market ❧

Compared to what it is today, New York City in the 1800s was a small town. Most days of the week you could find unemployed or retired men sitting in front of the market passing the time. John Lozier was a regular at the market. When he didn't appear for several days, the men wondered what had happened to him.

Finally, he returned, but he didn't seem to want to talk to anyone. The men were patient because they respected John and knew he would talk when he was ready. After about a week, he spoke in a solemn voice. "I've been meeting with our mayor. He's worried about the island of Manhattan. He thinks it might sink. There are too many tall buildings weighing it down."

The men all looked at each other, trying to determine whether they had heard John correctly. "That sounds crazy to me, John," one of them finally said.

John agreed, "It does seem strange, but I must admit the mayor is a pretty smart man ... and a good man, too. He's worried about people getting hurt and losing their homes."

Another man said, "Well, what does he think we ought to do?"

John replied, "Well, I think he's got a good plan. It'll be a lot of work, but we should be able to get it done. He wants us to go to the base of the island and saw it off, so it will be free to float. Then we'll row the island out to sea, turn it around, and then row it back into a better position and anchor it."

Before the men could offer any objections, John explained, "I am in charge of the project and will have to hire an army of men. Of course, you men are my friends, so you will get first pick of the jobs. The best paying jobs, of course, will be underwater. It's going to take a big crew to saw this island loose. The mayor says he'll give triple pay to the underwater crew."

The men hooted and hollered, "When are you going to choose?"

John answered, "I figured right now. If you're interested, line up, and I will time how long you can hold your breath." John carefully wrote each applicant's name in a book and followed it with how long he held his breath.

The next few weeks the market hummed with excitement. Finally, Lozier announced, "We're ready. There'll be a grand parade tomorrow with music and cheers. A day to celebrate a new New York City."

The day came. Five hundred to 1,000 people gathered. An hour passed and nothing happened. At first the crowd was fearful that perhaps a disaster had occurred. When the second hour passed, there were a few who realized they had been tricked. After three hours, even the most enthusiastic about saving Manhattan Island by sawing off its roots realized they had just witnessed a hoax.

❦ Indian Summer ❦

When a misty haze hangs on the horizon and Autumn brings crisp, cold days followed by days of warm and wonderful sunshine, we say, "It's Indian Summer." But how did it get such a name?

Early accounts tell us that a smoky haze identified this time of year more than a sudden spurt of warm weather. It's possible because long ago this was the time of year Indians prepared for winter by burning grass to clear and fertilize their land. Sometimes the Indians would use fire to drive animals out of the forest for one more big hunt before cold weather set in. Autumn was also the time for harvest celebrations which included powwows with dancing, singing and pipe ceremonies in the red glow of huge fires.

So, if after a cold spell this Autumn the weather warms and there's a haze on the horizon, think about the Indians and how Indian Summers came to be. [United States]

NOVEMBER

November

Birds have gone south.
The sky's slate gray.
The earth is bare.
The trees, passé.
Days are shortened.
Nights are long.
Clouds are thick.
Wind's too strong.
Sensible bears have gone to sleep.
Papers announce: Snow will be deep!
Forgotten are Fall's bright blazes,
Her Joseph coat and misty hazes.
Perched between earth's life and death,
November cries with shortened breath.

—Pat Nelson

❦ Man and Bird ❧

A man with a shotgun said to a game bird, "It is all nonsense, you know, about hunting being a cruel sport. I put my skill with a shotgun against your cunning. That is all there is to it. It seems to me that it is a fair game."

"True," said the bird, "but I don't wish to play."

"Why not?" inquired the man with the shotgun.

"The game," the bird replied, "is fair as you say. The chances are about even, but consider the prize. I am in the game for you, but what is there in the game for me?"

Not being prepared with an answer, the man with the shotgun wisely removed his bullets. [Ambrose Bierce]

❦ Señor Coyote, the Judge ❧

"Help me! Help me!" came a call from a ditch where Señor Rattlesnake was caught underneath a large rock. Señor Rabbit heard the cry for help as he hopped down the road, and he found Señor Rattlesnake in his predicament. "Rattlesnake," he called. "Can I help you?"

"Yes, you can. Can you get this rock off of me? I can't move." Señor Rabbit was afraid of Señor Rattlesnake, but he couldn't bear to see anyone suffer, not even his enemies. So he pushed and pushed and pushed on the stone until Señor Rattlesnake was free.

"You did well," said Señor Rattlesnake, "and now I'll reward you."

Señor Rabbit said, "It was nothing. I'm glad you're okay."

"Yes, you do need a reward," hissed Señor Rattlesnake as he began to coil.

"What are you doing?" a frightened Señor Rabbit said.

Señor\Rattlesnake hissed, "I'm going to eat you. That is your reward."

"But I just saved your life!" cried Señor Rabbit. At that moment Señor Coyote came walking by. Señor Rattlesnake and Señor Rabbit screamed out their stories to Señor Coyote, who was a judge.

Señor Coyote thought for a moment and then said, "Do you both agree that Señor Rattlesnake was under that stone?" They both nodded their heads. "Then Señor Rattlesnake, I want you to get back under that stone so I can see how everything was." Señor Rattlesnake agreed, and Señor Coyote rolled the stone onto his back.

"Is that just the way you were?" asked Señor Coyote.

Señor Rattlesnake hissed, "Yes. Now get this stone off my back."

"I have a better idea," said the judge. "Stay right where you are. That's your reward for being unkind to Señor Rabbit, who helped you." [Mexico]

❧ Turkey Girl ☙

Yellow Corn Girl and Turkey Girl were sisters. Turkey Girl was the youngest and spent all her days taking care of the turkeys. When it came time in the Fall for the great feast and Indian dance, their parents took Yellow Corn Girl with them, but Turkey Girl had to stay at home and do her work.

The turkeys asked, "Why don't you go, too?"

"I have no moccasins," she answered. "I don't have any beads either. There are so many things I don't have." Turkey Girl began to cry.

"You shall have everything," said the turkeys. They shook their wings and out fell a beautiful shawl, a bright blue belt, and a lovely pair of moccasins. Now Turkey Girl had all she needed.

She went to the pavilion by herself, stood in a corner, and watched the dancers. Her sister and her mother saw her.

"Where did you get those clothes?" they scolded. They looked and sounded so mean that Turkey Girl ran home crying.

At home she decided to run away. When she told the turkeys, they said, "We will go, too. We no longer like it here."

They escorted Turkey Girl to a lake and then she said, "Goodbye. You go to the mountains to live, and I am going to live here."

Her family never found Turkey Girl or the turkeys, and to this day the mountains of New Mexico are full of wild turkeys. [Native American]

❧ Good Land, Big Potatoes ☙

In the Snake River valley lives an old-timer who is known as Old Jim. Occasionally, Old Jim comes to town to strut around and brag about how fertile his land is. When you talk to him though, he admits he can't market what he grows. He started with pumpkins, but they grew so big he couldn't lift them up onto his wagon. Then he switched to growing potatoes.

Old Jim's potatoes grew very big, and a couple of years ago, the director of a nearby boys' camp went to Old Jim to buy 100 pounds of potatoes. Jim scratched his head. "Only a hundred pounds?" he asked. Before the fellow could answer, Jim said, "I'm sure sorry. I just can't do it. I'm just not going to cut a potato in two." [United States]

❧ The Worst Storm ❧

It had been an unusually warm Minnesota Fall, but on November 11, 1940, Armistice Day, a holiday we now call Veterans Day, there was an unforgettable storm. The Anderson family awakened to three inches of snow and a brisk wind that created a windchill factor of 32 degrees below zero.... And then the weather turned ugly, culminating in 63-mile-per-hour wind gusts, an actual temperature of 6 degrees above zero, and about 2 feet of snow. Minnesotans are accustomed to larger snowfalls, but the wind whipping and drifting the snow made this storm the most dangerous one in Minnesota history.

Because of the warm Fall, the Anderson family had not taken their turkeys into the barn for the Winter. Instead, the turkeys had been roosting in the trees about three-quarters of a mile from the house. When the storm was over, the Andersons took their plow into the woods. The first thing they saw was a turkey's tail sticking out of the snow. The youngest Anderson said, "Well, there's one that's gone." He grabbed its tail to pull it out of the snow and the turkey flapped its wings. Nearly scared that boy to death. The turkey was alive because it had been insulated by the snow.

Everywhere the Andersons looked they saw tree limbs heavy with snow, but no turkeys. However, when they poked around in the snow with sticks, those turkeys stuck their heads up like jacks-in-the-box. The Andersons weren't that fortunate with all of their turkeys, though. A good many froze, so the Anderson women canned them and sold them for 25 cents each.

Not all turkey farmers were as fortunate as the Anderson family. Because it was the opening weekend of hunting season, many farmers were sitting in boats in duck blinds when the storm hit. Most did not get back home during the storm to care for their turkeys, and some animals were lost forever because of the blinding snow.

One farmer found 30 of his sheep frozen in ice so thick he had to get a hatchet to break them loose. Some cattle froze in the fields. Some died of suffocation because their nostrils froze. And pigs with frozen tails had them broken off by farmers using them as handles to pull the porkers out of drifts. But, by far, the greatest loss was the turkeys. Many a farmer had his whole flock wiped out.

Today in Minnesota if it is snowing in the morning and the snow has not stopped by 3:00 in the afternoon, everything closes. People go home while they are still able to travel. Those who lived through the Armistice Day storm are the first to leave, especially the turkey farmers, and they are followed by those who have heard stories about the worst storm in Minnesota history.

Grateful acknowledgment is made to William H. Hull for permission to retell "The Women Who Canned 200 Jars of Turkey," p. 68, in his copyrighted material, *All Hell Broke Loose*.

❧ The Boy with a Dream ❧

Harry loved to play the piano. He even loved to practice. When he was 13 he took lessons from his next-door neighbor. Soon he was playing better than she. His next teacher, Mrs. E. C. White, was a fine pianist who taught Harry well. And when he was 15, she introduced him to Paderewski, a great Polish pianist.

Harry was afraid to meet such a famous artist, but Paderewski's smile was warm and his words were gentle. Harry soon found the courage to ask this great man how to play a certain part of the Minuet in G. Paderewski was obviously pleased with the question and went to the piano to demonstrate his answer. When he was certain Harry knew how it should be played, he stood and invited Harry to the piano. When Harry finished the minuet and saw the smile on Paderewski's face, he knew he had done well. He also knew that he wanted more than anything else to become the greatest pianist in the world.

The very next year hard times hit Harry's family. Harry's father lost everything in the grain market in Kansas City. Not only did Harry have to give up his dream of becoming a concert pianist, but he had to work long hours to help his family which left him no time for daily practice. The piano became less and less important in his life.

Harry worked in a drugstore, as a clerk at the *Kansas City Star*, as a time-keeper for a railroad construction gang, and as a bank clerk. Finally, he came back to his father's farm and worked there.

Eventually, Harry found his way into politics. He must have been pretty good at what he did, because he became the 33rd president of the United States, Harry S. Truman.

❧ Two Foolish Cats ❧

A long time ago in Japan, a big cat and a little cat were friends. One morning they each found a wonderfully fresh rice cake. When they compared their cakes, they found that the little cat had a large cake and the big cat had a tiny cake.

The big cat pouted, "I am bigger. I should have the big cake."

But the little cat growled and showed his teeth. "That is not so. I am small. I need more food to grow."

They argued and fussed and finally decided to go see Monkey, to have him divide the cakes evenly. They found him sitting on a branch, with a golden scale and wearing a red hat. When they explained their argument, Monkey smiled, "I shall put an end to it."

He put a rice cake on each side of his scale. Of course, it didn't balance because the big rice cake was heavier. He picked up the big cake, took a bite out of it, and then put it back on the scale. "That should make them equal," he said. But he had taken too big a bite. Now the small cake was heavier. So Monkey took a bite out of the small cake, and then the large cake was again heavier.

The big cat said, "Ahem, sir, I think you've eaten enough."

"Yes," said the little cat. "They're even enough."

But the monkey ate until both rice cakes were gone. Then he smiled at the cats, "Now you have nothing to quarrel about."

The two cats went slinking down the road, feeling foolish, hungry, and, would you believe, tired of arguing? In fact, it is said that they never argued again. [Japan]

❦ The Animal Lover ❧

Jane Goodall had always loved animals. Even when she was a preschooler, she not only loved playing with them but also taking care of them. She loved learning about their habits and abilities.

Once, when Jane was only four years old, she wanted to watch a hen lay an egg. She very quietly slipped into an empty chicken house. She didn't tell anyone what she was doing for fear they'd disturb the hen. She'd tried this many times before, but each time the hen was interrupted. Consequently, the hen didn't lay an egg. That caused Jane to wonder whether hens wouldn't lay if they were disturbed by any kind of noise. This time she sat silently and alone. One…two…three…four hours passed. Finally, a hen came in and laid an egg. Jane jumped up and down and clapped her hands! She was so delighted. Now she knew for sure that hens won't lay if they are disturbed.

Jane never lost her love for or curiosity about animals. After she graduated from high school, she went to Africa to study. Chimpanzees became her subject every hour of the day. They became her life project. She didn't read books to learn about them. Instead, she lived with them. She played with them, and she watched them for hours. Gradually, they began to treat her as though she was one of them.

No one had actually lived this close to chimps before Jane went to Africa. Before her research, scientists believed big animals lived on fruits and vegetables, a few insects and rodents. Jane found they also ate animals as large as pigs or monkeys, and were capable of making tools. They stripped branches and used them to catch termites in their mounds. And sometimes, to the surprise of Jane and many other scientists, the chimpanzees would take on another tribe and kill them off.

Dr. Jane Goodall has rewritten the textbook on chimps and brought new respect for them all over the world. When children ask her how they can train to have a life like she has had, she tells them they must have a body strong enough to withstand unusual environmental conditions in uncivilized areas, and they must love their subject and want to read everything that's printed about it.

❧ Snoozing Bears ❧

Have you ever wondered why bears hibernate in the Winter? They miss breakfast, lunch, and dinner for sometimes as long as seven months. Wouldn't you think they'd die from hunger?

But bears don't starve because in the Fall they eat large quantities of food. Some gain an extra 100 pounds or more. Then, when the weather gets cold and there isn't any food to be found, they climb into their cave, burrow, or hollowed out tree and snuggle down in their bed of leaves and grass. They sleep for weeks at a time. They can do this because their bodies are nourished by all the fat they gained in the Fall.

Bears have huge appetites, eating fish, insects, berries, nuts, roots, small animals, and honey when they can find it. Bears particularly love honey. Sometimes when they are raiding a hive, they swallow bees whole. Hunters have found as many as two quarts of stinging bees in a bear's stomach.

Also, the Indians of the Winnebago Bear Clan say bears suck their feet while they sleep, just as a baby sucks its thumb. Because bears walk on berries all Summer, crushing them into their feet, they are able to get nourishment from this sucking.

What is most remarkable about female bears is that they give birth in the Winter to two or three cubs that weigh less than one pound apiece and have no fur. As their mother sleeps, the cubs drink her milk. By the time she awakens for good in the Spring, they may weigh as much as eight pounds!

Scientists know a lot about bears, but they are still puzzled about how the bears know when it is time to prepare a new den for their Winter sleep. They never sleep in the same den twice. Maybe someday a boy or girl will grow up and be so curious about bears that he or she will want to learn everything there is to know about them. Jane Goodall, a Britisher, was so curious about chimps that before she even started college, she studied them in their own environment. Now she probably knows more about chimps than almost anyone else in the world.

❧ The Indian Cranberry ❧

Do you like cranberries? Most people think Thanksgiving would not be complete without them. These sour red berries that grew in bogs* near the Pilgrims' settlement on Cape Cod were strange to them. The Indians called the berries *ibimi*, which means berry. They showed the settlers why they liked the berries.

The Indians showed the Pilgrims how to make cranberry poultices** to draw out the venom*** when they were wounded. They taught the Pilgrims how to mix cranberries, fat, and dried venison to make a food called pemmican. The settlers were especially happy to find that the juice made a good red dye.

The settlers on Cape Cod used to tell a story about an Indian medicine man who was very good at casting spells. He cast one on a male Pilgrim and then stood him in quicksand. The medicine man began boasting to the Pilgrim about how good he was at casting spells. In fact, he bragged about all kinds of powers he had over nature. In spite of being trapped in quicksand, the Pilgrim got so angry that he began arguing with the Indian. He wanted the Indian to know that he was a pretty powerful man, too. At the end of 15 days they were still arguing. The Pilgrim was so weak from hunger, he thought he would have to give in when a white dove brought him a bright red berry. The grateful man hoped the dove would bring more, but of course there was the risk the Indian might cast a spell on the bird.

The dove did come back, over and over, with his mouth chock full of cranberries, and the man survived.

While all of this occurred, a red berry dropped to the ground and started the first cranberry bog. The Pilgrims loved the berries and thought they looked like the head of a crane. And that's why they named the berry "cranberry." [Native American]

---

*   bog: wet, spongy ground

**   poultice: a soft, usually heated, and sometimes medicated mass applied to sores

*** venom: magic charm, drug, or poison

❧ The Two Friends ❧

Once there were two men who were neighbors. They had been friends for years and prided themselves on never having argued. But then a trickster decided to have some fun. He made a coat that was red on the right side and blue on the left side.

One morning both friends were in their fields working. The trickster walked by each one, showing a different side of his coat. At noon the friends met under a tree to eat lunch.

"Did you see that man who walked through our fields this morning?" asked one.

"Yup."

"He sure had a bright coat. What color was it?"

"Blue."

"Blue! It was red."

"Nonsense, it wasn't red. It was blue."

"Man, you're a fool."

"You say you're my friend and yet you call me a fool."

The men started to fight, but their wives stopped them. The women found the trickster and his bright coat. When they told their husbands, the men became friends again—and I think they still are! [Africa]

❧ Thanksgiving Turkey ❧

A long time ago families often served wild turkey for Thanksgiving dinner. Jimmy Jones, a young scrawny kid, wanted to bring a wild turkey home to his mom. So he hid by the corn crib hoping to catch a big one when the birds arrived to eat. All at once, a whole flock of turkeys landed. Jimmy rushed out from behind the corn crib into the middle of the flock. He moved quickly and grabbed two just as the whole flock decided this wasn't a safe place to eat. They all took off like a huge airplane with a very scared boy hanging onto the legs of the two turkeys he had grabbed.

Jimmy didn't want to let go. He knew his mom would love having a real old-fashioned Thanksgiving dinner. Because the turkeys were strong and able to fly fast, the boy almost lost his grip when he realized how he could survive and still have turkey. He let one bird go and held onto the other bird with both hands. That slowed down the turkey. Jimmy was not a big child, but he was a pretty big load for one bird. It wasn't long before the turkey was too tired to fly and they landed.

When Jimmy came home with his turkey, the family really appreciated the boy's effort. However, when he told the story of how he caught the bird, they didn't believe a word of it. Six generations later the Jones family is still telling the tale on Thanksgiving and everyone believes it, or at least, pretends to. [American Tall Tale]

❧ Chinese Marvels ❧

A man from northern China began a long trip south to view the monstrous carrots he had heard about. On the way he met a man from the south who was on his way to the north to view their marvelous bridges. While discussing their trips with each other they realized that if the man from the north could describe its bridges in a way the man from the south could understand, and the southern gentleman could describe the carrots so the northerner could picture them in his mind, each would save himself a long walk.

The northerner said, "We had a bridge accident some time ago. A man fell into the water."

The southerner answered, "Well, go on. I want to know what the bridge looks like."

"Oh, I can't," said the northerner. "He hasn't hit the water yet."

"Hmmm," said the southerner, "That's a mighty high bridge, but our carrots are just as unusual. When we dig out our carrots and lay them on the ground next summer, you won't have to picture them in your mind. You'll actually be able to see them because they'll reach all the way to the north." [China]

DECEMBER

December Tale

There once was a little old woman
Who polished the stars.
Perched on top of the mountain
At the darkest time of the year,
In the misty dawn
Before the sun was awake,
She plucked them from the heavens
Until her basket overflowed.
Back in her kitchen
She scrubbed and stacked,
Shined and buffed,
Until she saw her distorted image
In their mirrored brilliance.
She saw herself when young,
Always stretching and grabbing for
    the stars,
Not to scrub and polish,
But to pin to her heart like a medal.
Some girls pinned roses,
But she wanted the world's notice.

Today, there was no acclaim
For her self-appointed duties.
But she had her satisfaction.
Contentedly, each evening, she carried
Her dazzling basket back up the
    mountain,
Hung her pointed diamonds
Into the still pink sky,
Replenishing it with exquisite
    incentives
For young people to notice
And reach for.

—Pat Nelson

45

❦ The Winter Solstice ❧

It was the darkest time of the year, when the world was very young. In the far north country, days were short. Winds were strong and bitter cold. A tribe huddled around its fire, fearing the sun would never return. The chief, understanding the dread that the darkest time brings, got to his feet and shouted, "Make torches! Everyone follow me!"

With long sticks of fire brightening the dark night, they followed their chief up the mountain, single file. The wild howls of the wolves and snow so deep they could hardly walk made some beg to go back. But the chief urged them on.

Those who remembered the trip from past years tried to comfort the frightened ones. A young man began to sing like a lone bird. And then another man joined him. And another, until they all joined to sing an old tribal song. When it was over, there was a hush, until a wolf howl broke the silence. The whole tribe forgot their fear and roared in laughter at the wolf's poor attempt at singing.

The rest of the way up the mountain their spirits soared as they sang together. At the top, the chief ordered them to hold their torches high. "We are going to tease the sun to shine," he cried. They all stretched high and waved their flames. When the eastern sky began to lighten, they cheered and shouted. But when that orange ball finally peeked above the horizon, and they were assured the sun had returned, tears rolled down their cheeks, and they fell to their knees in praise. [Pat Nelson]

❦ Reindeer and Whale ❧

It was Spring in the far north country. There were no green sprouts yet, only snow and ice beginning to melt. Reindeer was walking along the shore when he heard Whale shout, "Hey, Reindeer! How about a little fun? Would you play tug-of-war with me?" Reindeer thought it was a wonderful idea.

Whale chose to make a rope for himself out of seaweed. Reindeer made his out of grass. When the ropes were long enough, they joined them. Reindeer took the end of his and tied it around his body. Whale tied his around his tail. The game was on!

Reindeer pulled hard toward the land, but the tundra* was so soft from melted snow that he sank in it to his knees.

The water gushed as Whale's tail slapped the sea. And when he saw Reindeer bogged down in soft earth, Whale was certain he would win. His tail made an extra hard tug on the rope and the rope snapped! Whale was thrust to the ocean bottom, while Reindeer went flying across the tundra.

I don't know if Whale is still playing tug-of-war, but I do know that Reindeer never goes near the ocean. [Eskimo]

---

* tundra: a level or rolling, treeless plain, typical of arctic and subarctic areas

❧ Friendship Without Envy ❧

A sociable nightingale was looking for friendship. She flew in and out of the trees in the forest and found not one friend, but only singers filled with envy. Perhaps I shall find a friend outside of the forest, she thought, and she flew trustingly toward a farm where she found a peacock in the garden.

"Beautiful peacock, I admire you!" she crooned.

"I admire you, too, lovely nightingale!"

"Let's be friends," said the nightingale. "We won't have to envy each other, for you are as lovely to the eye as I am to the ear."

The peacock agreed with the nightingale, and so they became good friends.

The point: Sometimes the best and most lasting friendships are formed by people who have complementary gifts and dispositions. [Gotthold Ephraim Lessing]

❧ The Baker's Dozen ❧

Many years ago in Albany, New York, Master Van Amsterdam always baked cookies shaped like St. Nicholas for the holidays. They were very popular all over the Thirteen Colonies.

One Christmas Eve, after a very hard day's work, Van Amsterdam finally locked the door so he could count his money. But before he started, a very ugly woman banged on the door and demanded to be let in. Inside, she yelled, "I want a dozen St. Nicholas cookies!" Master Van Amsterdam wrapped up 12 cookies and tied the package with a string. The woman said, "You only gave me 12—I want 13."

Master Van Amsterdam did not want to argue, but he said, "You and I both know that a dozen is 12 and not 13. I'm not giving you one more cookie. Now, go!"

The ugly woman said, "You've cheated me! You'll be sorry. I will not forget it!"

The next week, everything went wrong. The St. Nicholas cookies were bewitched. No matter what he did, they either stuck to the roof of his mouth or were too hard to chew. Some stuck to the pans like glue. Van Amsterdam began losing his customers to other bakeries. Then one day, he sat down and thought about what had happened. If he had been more generous with the woman, he wouldn't be having this trouble. He made a decision. From that day forward, Van Amsterdam, the baker, would always make a dozen with 13.

The next morning, the ugly woman was his first customer. When Van Amsterdam gave her 13 cookies, she said, "Fine. From now on, I won't haunt you." And it became the custom in the colonies to give 13 instead of 12, which is known as a baker's dozen. [United States]

❧ The Spiders' Gift ❧

The presents were wrapped and the tree was trimmed with bright balls and toys. Mother, Father, Susan, and John had gone to bed. Everyone was asleep except the spiders.

When the clock struck 12:00, hundreds of mother spiders, father spiders, and teeny, tiny baby spiders came out of their secret hiding places. They crawled up the trunk of the Christmas tree and all over its branches, leaving their special gift.

In the morning the children screamed, "Look at the tree!"

Mother and Father came running into the living room. When they saw the tree, they cried, "Oh!" They had never seen such a beautiful tree! It glittered. It shimmered. It sparkled with tinsel that shone through clouds of angels' hair.

What they didn't know and never found out was that the tinselled webs silvering the tree had been left by the little gray, furry spiders. [Germany]

❧ The Shoemaker and the Elves ❧

One night, a very poor shoemaker cut out two pairs of shoes before he and his wife went to bed. He left them on his sewing table in his shop. "I'll sew them the first thing in the morning. Maybe we'll have money for Christmas, if I can sell them," he said to his wife just before they drifted to sleep.

In the morning, the shoemaker was shocked to find that the two pairs of shoes he had left to work on were already finished! They had been sewn together with the finest of stitches.

He and his wife could not understand it. The shoes were sewn so well that they had no trouble at all selling both pairs that day. That night, the shoemaker cut out three pairs of shoes to work on the next morning.

The next morning there were three pairs of finely-sewn, brand-new shoes on the shoemaker's work table! The little shoemaker and his wife were so happy they danced around the shop. And once again, they sold all that the workers had sewn together.

They became curious. Who could be treating them so kindly? They thought about it all day. That night they both decided to hide in the shop to find out who was being so good to them. They hadn't been hiding in the closet very long when two little old elves, as naked as jaybirds, came sneaking in the front door.

The next day was Christmas Eve. The shoemaker and his wife wanted to give the elves something for all the elves had done for them. By nightfall, the shoemaker's wife had made new outfits for the elves: little green pants, red coats, and black hats.

That night they laid the suits and hats on the table and hid in the closet. After a bit, the door opened slowly and the naked, shivering little elves climbed up on the work table. When they saw the little suits, they giggled with excitement and could hardly get them on quickly enough. Then they hopped onto the floor and danced all around the shop. Just before they danced out the door, they waved and shouted, "Merry Christmas!" And then they were gone, never to return.

The shoemaker and his wife had the best Christmas they ever had, and from that day forward they were able to make and sell many pairs of shoes. [Germany]

❦ How Robin's Breast Became Red ❧

When the world was young, in the cold, far north, there was only one fire. A hunter and his son kept it going. They kept it safe from North Bear, who wanted the north all to himself.

One day the hunter became ill. His son nursed him and kept the fire going, while North Bear watched from behind a tree. Night after night the boy forced himself to stay awake and guard the fire. But finally one night, exhausted, he was overcome by sleep. Quickly, North Bear jumped on the fire with his wet paws and rolled upon it until he thought it was out. Then he ran away, laughing.

A little gray robin, perched on a branch, saw it all. When North Bear had gone, he darted down to what remained of the fire. Quickly, he searched until he found a tiny live coal. He hovered just above it, fanning it with his wings. His little breast was scorched red, but even then he didn't stop. Not until a fine, red flame burst forth from the ashes did he feel his job was done.

The flame spread and soon the whole north country was lit again. The fire was so bright that the people of the south could see red and blue northern lights in the sky.

North Bear went back to his cave, knowing he would never have the north land to himself. Even today, people all over the world love to tell their children how the robin's breast became red. [Native American]

❦ The Young Fox and the Old Fox ❧

A young fox was mesmerized watching the birds in the sky fly to and fro. "Father," he called. "Father, I want to fly."

The father, a bit irritated with his irrational son, said, "Fly? Where will you get your wings? From an angel?" The old fox laughed a bit. He liked his joke.

The young fox, however, was determined to fulfill his dream. He made himself a pair of wings out of hen feathers. Then he climbed a high tower and threw himself out the window. Not a great flyer, this novice airman fell to the ground.

The old fox, who had been watching, ran to him. "How did you get on with your flying?" he asked his son.

"The flying," answered the young fox, "was as smooth as anything could be, Father. But the landing ... the landing needs some improvement."

"Serves you right," said his father. "You always think you are so much smarter than the old. Not only are we wiser than you because of our experience, but we also know that when you don't have wings, it isn't in the cards for you to fly."

The young fox said nothing and limped away. [Austria]

❧ The Horse and the Colt ❧

A widower horse chose to raise his son in a perfect meadow for horses. The colt loved it. But because he was young, he wasted it. He stuffed himself with grasses, wasted his time, galloped for no reason, and rested when he wasn't tired.

The colt grew lazy and fat. Finally, disgusted with life, he said to his father, "For some time now, I've not been well. The grass gives me indigestion. The clover no longer smells sweet. And the air bothers my lungs. In short, I am certain that I will die unless we leave."

The father replied, "Since it is a matter of life and death, we will leave."

The old horse led his son up and down arid mountains. The grass was gone, every tuft of it. After several days of hunger, hard walking, and no food, the colt could hardly drag his legs. He complained he was dying. However, the old horse forced him to continue.

As soon as the old horse thought the lesson had been learned, he returned to the old meadow by a road unknown to the colt. When the young horse caught sight of the green grass, he ate all he could. "I believe, Father, this is the best grass I have ever eaten. I knew you'd find a better place for us to live. We can stay here, can't we?" The old horse nodded in agreement.

After his stomach was filled, the colt ran around and around the field. Then it came to him. He recognized his very own home. He was embarrassed, but his father nudged him a little bit with his nose. "He who enjoys too much is soon disgusted with pleasure. To be happy, one must be moderate," the father said gently. [France]

❧ Why the Evergreen ❧

Long, long ago, when the plants and trees were young, the Great Indian Spirit told them to stay awake and keep watch for seven nights. At first, they all stayed awake. But each night a few more gave up the watch and fell asleep.

On the seventh night when the Great Indian Spirit came back to see who had stayed awake, his heart was warmed when he saw that the pine, the spruce, the fir, the holly, and the laurel had all managed to keep watch for seven nights. He said, "You have endured, and because of your strength to endure, I am giving you the gift of eternal greenness."

From that day on most trees would turn brilliant colors in the Fall and then lose their leaves until warm Spring sun and rain encouraged new leaves to form. But the trees that had the strength to endure would be forever green, every season of the year. [Native American]

❧ Greed ❧

A poor man one day met an old friend who had become a holy man. The poor man complained and complained about his state of poverty. After hearing his friend complain endlessly about his sad state of affairs, the holy man said, "Watch me," and then pointed at a brick at the side of the road. That brick immediately turned into gold. The holy man picked it up and gave it to his poor friend. The poor friend said, "Thank you," but it was obvious he was not terribly impressed.

As they walked, they passed a public building and the poor man saw a lion statue. He said, "Could you turn that into gold?" The holy man did, but the fact that he had performed this magnificent feat did not seem to impress his friend at all.

Exasperated, the holy man said, "What more do you want?"

The friend answered, "I have seen you point at a brick and point at a lion, and they both turned to gold. You ask me what I want? I want your finger." [India]

❧ Hadrian ❧

Hadrian, one of the Roman emperors, was out for a ride on his horse one sunny morning. As his horse galloped down the road, Hadrian looked out across a field and saw an old man digging a ditch. Hadrian stopped his horse and called, "Hey, old man, you look too old to be working so hard." After a pause the emperor said with a laugh, "I guess you spent too much time being foolish when you were young, and now it has caught up with you." Hadrian paused again and squinted his eyes in order to see better what was going on. "What are you doing in that ditch?" he called.

Slowly, the old man stood. His hair was white and his face deeply wrinkled, but when he recognized the emperor his face broke into a smile. "Good morning, sir," he said. "You wish to know what I am doing? I'm planting fig trees." As he spoke, his smile seemed to stretch broader. "I'm afraid you are wrong about my youth. I have always worked hard. Work is sweet, and besides, I love figs."

"Well, that's all well and good," said Hadrian, "but tell me, how old are you?"

The old man seemed to stretch taller as he answered, "I celebrated my 100th birthday a few weeks ago."

"Well, that's a good age, old man," said Hadrian, "but do you really think you are going to live long enough to see these trees produce figs?"

"Maybe I will and maybe I won't," said the old man with a little laugh, "but it doesn't matter because I plant the trees for my children and my grandchildren to enjoy after I am gone, just like my parents planted for me."

Hadrian looked pleased as he said, "Would you do me a favor old man? If you live to see the first harvest of your figs, would you bring me some? I love figs, too." And, of course, the old man said he would.

And he did live. Five years later the old man and his wife had their first harvest. They filled a basket with the biggest, juiciest figs and the old man proudly carried it to the emperor's palace. The emperor was delighted with the gift and invited the old man to sit and share some fruit with him. When they had their fill, the emperor told his treasurer to empty the basket into their fruit bowl and fill the basket with gold for the old man.

The treasurer looked strained as he went to fill the basket. When he returned, he set the basket on the floor and whispered in the emperor's ear, "This man is a Jew. Have you forgotten? We Romans haven't trusted Jews for centuries. Are you sure you want to give this man a gift?"

The emperor pulled away from the treasurer's face and looked up at him. "You do not understand. This man is over 100 years old. He still believes that work is sweet and plants fig trees for his children and grandchildren. It makes no difference what religion he is. He is a good man and deserves a basket of gold." [Jewish Folklore]

❦ The Fly ❧

One morning a fly shivered with fear when it saw a swallow. "There is nothing more cruel than a swallow," it cried. "They give a fly one look and in the next instant that fly is gone. I'm getting out of here."

The fly flew quickly into the stable where it felt safe until it discovered a nasty spider in every corner, just waiting for a fly to become tangled in its web. The fly scolded itself for its stupidity. "I should have known that dirty stable would not be safe," it said, and immediately winged towards the palace.

"Oh, what a beautiful palace! Surely, this will be a clean safe place to live," the fly said. Nevertheless, the fly was cautious and spent the afternoon investigating every corner until it was convinced there were no swallows or spiders.

That evening after sunset the servants lit candles in every room. As the fly flew from one candle to the next, it was dazzled by the flames. "How enchanting this is! Now I can enjoy the night as well as the day," it tittered. "With this beauty and no swallows or spiders, I'll be able to relax."

The fly became so relaxed in its new home that it didn't notice how the candlelight seemed to cast a spell on him. Night after night the fly was compelled to soar closer and closer to the dancing fire. One night it flew so near a flame its wingtips were singed, and the fly fell to the ground never to get up again.

And what is the lesson? Beware of enchantments, sometimes they disguise danger. [England]

❦ The Blind Man and the Lame Man ❧

A blind man, having lost his way, happened to stumble against a lame man who could not make it up onto the road.

"Help me, good fellow, onto the road," said the blind man.

"How can I do that?" asked the crippled man. "I guess you are blind and can't see that I am unable to make it up this little hill to the road because of my lame legs."

The blind man thought for a moment and then said, "I have a strong back and two sturdy legs, but my blindness continually causes me to be lost. Why don't I carry you on my back? You can direct me where to go."

And so the two men hurried along the road laughing and talking about the new company they had just formed. One was the director, the other was the transportation department. [Africa]

January

January, Janus's* namesake,
Looks both ways.
He winks at the errors
Of the year just passed,
But looks the new year
Straight in the eye.

—Pat Nelson

*Janus: a two-faced Roman god who always looked both ways. He was the keeper of doors and gates, which is why we associate him with beginnings.

❧ Cold Tall Tales ❧

Minnesota has long been known for its cold Winters. One year in Rochester a hotel caught on fire in the middle of the night during one of the coldest Winters Minnesota had ever known. Ed was trapped in his room on the third floor. He didn't know what to do until he spied a pitcher of water on the dresser. He ran to the window with the pitcher and poured the water out in a long stream. It was so cold that night that the water froze as it fell, and Ed slid to the ground on an icicle.

But Minnesota isn't the only state that experiences cold weather. Temperatures drop quite low in Pennsylvania, too. One year firefighters left their station to put out a barn fire in the middle of Winter. Right after they arrived, a freight train was passing on the tracks nearby, and the crew stopped to help extinguish the fire. They fetched large buckets from the fire engine, filled them with water, and threw the water at the barn. But it was so cold that by the time they got to the blazing barn, the steaming hot water had frozen solid in the buckets. However, the water had frozen so rapidly that the ice was still warm. Unfortunately, there was no way to put out the fire, and the barn burned to the ground. [American Tall Tale]

❦ Ivan and Maryushka ❧

It had been snowing since early morning. Ivan and Maryushka watched Winter lay its white carpet over everything. How pure it looked—not a footprint anywhere. They were old now and dreaded the harshness of the Russian Winter, but still loved its beauty.

In late afternoon the snow stopped, and the neighborhood children came to play in their yard. Ivan and Maryushka had never had a child, and even now they still yearned for a little girl. As they watched the children, Ivan said, "Come, Maryushka, let us play in the snow, too. It looks like fun."

Maryushka scowled. "You are a fool. I am too old to play in the snow ... and so are you!" But in the end, she went outside and played.

When the children began making a snowman, Ivan called to her, "Maryushka, let's make a snowgirl." She agreed and they began rolling little snowballs into big ones. When three big balls were properly placed, Ivan went inside and found an old bonnet and apron and dressed the snowgirl. Then Maryushka brought out two coals for eyes, a carrot for its nose, and a long string of beads to go around its neck. The old couple couldn't stop smiling at their wonderful snowgirl.

As the sun slipped behind the trees, the children left. "It's time for supper," Ivan said, "but before we say goodbye to the little one, let us give her a name."

Maryushka immediately spoke. "Snegourka has always been my favorite." Ivan agreed.

The two little old people waved as they said, "Goodbye, Snegourka," and, wonder of wonders, Snegourka came to life!

"Please let me live with you. I love you both," she cried. Ivan and Maryushka didn't hesitate. They were delighted to bring her into their home.

Snegourka was the delight of the old couple's life all Winter. They taught her Russian games and songs. The three of them danced by the fire and forgot all about the harsh Winter.

All went well until the Spring equinox. When the sun became stronger, Snegourka became cheerless. When she became cross, they wondered if she was ill. One day, during a warm Spring rain, Snegourka went outside and sat under a great big oak tree. She sat there until she melted away with the rest of the snow. Ivan and Maryushka cried and cried. They missed her so much.

Seasons move on, one after another. The world never stops. Spring turned into Summer, and Summer, into Fall. When Autumn leaves covered the ground, Ivan and Maryushka went out to rake them. Suddenly, a cold wind blew across the old woman's face. She stood up quickly and called, "Ivan, Ivan! I feel Winter! It is coming back. Maybe Snegourka will come back, too!" [Russia]

❦ Reynard the Fox ❧

Reynard, the tricky fox, watched a fisherman put a whole string of fish onto the back of his cart. Then the man whipped his horse and hurried home.

Reynard was hungry and wanted those fish, so he ran ahead of the cart. When he was far enough ahead, he lay down in the road and played dead. The fisherman, seeing the dead fox, picked him up and threw him onto the back of the cart. All the way home the fisherman dreamed of the money he would have when he skinned the fox and sold his fur. The fisherman talked on and on to himself of being rich as a king, living in a castle trimmed with gold and silver, and having hundreds of servants. All this because of that beautiful fox fur in the back of his cart.

Of course, Reynard had been busy eating. When he finished the last fish, he tapped the fisherman on the shoulder and said, "I trust you will invite me to share your wealth." Then he jumped down and ran into the woods.

The fisherman screamed, "Stop! Stop! You're supposed to be dead. If I don't have your fur, I won't be rich." ... And, once more, Reynard showed how tricky he was. [France]

❧ Judy Blume ❧

Judy Blume the author, was born in 1938 and grew up in Elizabeth, New Jersey, enjoying life. She lived with her mother, who was shy and quiet, her father, who was a dentist, and her brother, who was four years older than she. But even in a wonderful family, sometimes children feel alone.

When Judy was a little girl, she was afraid to ask her parents questions about subjects that might embarrass them and herself, too. She was curious about her body and how it would change as she grew older. She wanted to talk to her parents about religion, especially God. She would love to have had the courage to tell her parents about the bad feelings she had sometimes, but she was afraid her feelings wouldn't be as nice as her mother expected. And because of the fears, the years passed with nothing discussed.

Judy was a good student and after high school, she graduated from college with a degree in education. When she found teaching would not fulfill her creative needs, she enrolled in a weekly writing course. She became so excited about writing a book that while she was in the course, she wrote a chapter each week. It was sort of like homework. After looking at her manuscript each week, her teacher would send her a note of encouragement that Judy would read over and over. When she completed the course, she enrolled again. This was the beginning of her writing career.

Did she sell that first book? Judy admits that it was not a very good book, but eventually, it sold. She continued writing, but was not really satisfied with her results until she recalled her own childhood. She remembered that she never liked the characters in the books she read then, because they seemed fake. She wanted characters that behaved and acted like she did. She wanted them to discuss the subjects that all kids want to know more about but are afraid to ask.

Because of her recollections, Judy Blume vowed she would never put a character in a book that didn't behave like a child in the real world. She has kept her word and written many books that help children understand life and themselves better. Some of them are: *Freckle Juice*, *Tales of a Fourth Grade Nothing*, *It's Not the End of the World*, *Are You There God? It's Me, Margaret*, *Superfudge*, *Judy Blume Diary: The Place to Put Your Own Feelings*, and many more.

❧ The Best Dream ❧

Once, three young men hired a cook and then went hunting. They hunted all day, but only came up with a partridge. Because a partridge is a small bird, it wouldn't make a meal for four hungry men. Instead, they decided to save it for breakfast. At that time, it would go to the man who dreamed the best dream.

They all went to sleep, and in the morning when they awakened, they were very hungry. So they immediately wanted to tell each other their dreams.

The first man confessed to a dream about the most beautiful princess in the world. The second man dreamed of his mother. The third man dreamed of heaven.

The fourth man was the cook. When it was his turn, he said, "As for me, I dreamed I ate the partridge, and I fear it must be true because I can't find it anywhere." [French Canada]

❧ A Real Kid's Story ❧

Gigi was only seven years old and already knew the joy of being snowed out of school. She and her neighborhood friends put on their heaviest clothes and went outside to investigate the heavy snow that had been dumped on Minneapolis. Streetcars and autos were stranded everywhere. There was so much snow that car owners used long sticks to shove down into the drifts hoping to find their lost vehicles. Tow trucks and plows were everywhere, trying to rescue vehicles once they were found. Most interesting was a Pepsi truck, half turned over, with bottles dumped into the snow. For some reason, Gigi's gang of friends thought it was perfectly all right to carry as much pop home as they could. The next day they learned the truth.

They were all sitting in Gigi's living room, listening to the radio, when a policeman came to the door and inquired about Gigi and her gang. He said, "I came to get the merchandise that you kids stole yesterday." Gigi never dreamed they would call bottles of pop "stolen merchandise." When the policeman called her innocent little neighborhood group "a gang of thieves" she was shocked.

That event put a dent in Gigi's memory 50 years ago. Of course, she laughs about it now. They weren't punished, but they were made aware that stealing wasn't acceptable, no matter what the situation. Still, for many years, when anyone mentioned the big snow, Gigi and her friends found it a painful memory.

Grateful acknowledgment is made to William H. Hull for permission to retell "Free Pepsi Cola," p. 79, in his copyrighted material, *All Hell Broke Loose*.

❧ Martin ☙

There once was a young black boy named Martin, who had two wonderful white playmates. One day the white boys' mothers decided their boys should not play with Martin anymore. They didn't have any reason to exclude Martin except that he was black.

Martin was so sad. He couldn't believe that he suddenly lost his two best friends. His mother tried to explain segregation to him. She tried to make it clear to him that black people and white people lived separately in special sections of town. Whites went to white restaurants and white movies, and blacks went to black restaurants and black movies. Then she took him in her arms and said, "You must always remember. You are as good as anyone."

When he was older, Martin's father took him to get some shoes. They walked into the store and sat down. The clerk came over and said, "I am sorry, but black people must sit in the back of the store."

Martin's father stood up and said, "Come along, Martin. We're leaving." And then, turning to the clerk, he said, "I'm very sorry, but we will have to get Martin's shoes somewhere where we receive the proper respect."

Martin Luther King, Jr., never forget those two incidents. In college Martin decided to be a minister like his father. While there, he was inspired by a man from India, Mahatma Gandhi. Gandhi was trying to help people who were not treated as equal citizens in his country by teaching them to love rather than to hate their enemies. Martin read every book Gandhi wrote and was convinced that Gandhi's message was a new way to freedom for oppressed people. Martin knew that his life must be spent as a leader who preached and taught his people to love and not be violent, but to continue the struggle for freedom.

Martin was a peaceful child who grew up to be a peaceful but determined leader. In spite of his commitment to preaching and teaching about love and non-violence, he was assassinated April 4, 1968. Most states in the United States celebrate his birthday as a national holiday on the third Monday in January. Martin Luther King, Jr., was born January 15, 1919.

❧ A Tall Story ❧

One very cold January day some boy scouts were having a Winter gathering at their camp on Birch Lake in the far north. It was unbearably cold when they arrived, and during the night the temperature dropped even further to 40 degrees below zero. But when the scout leader announced the next morning, "Breakfast is ready," the boys jumped up, scurried around, found their clothes and started down the road to where their leader was waiting.

As they walked, they began talking, but it was so cold, their conversation froze as it came out of their mouths. The frigid words fell clattering onto the icy road. One of the boys ran back to the dormitory and found a basket. They all worked hard picking up those frozen words and took turns carrying the basket on their way to breakfast.

In the warmth of the kitchen, the words melted. At first the boys had fun listening to their conversation, but when they heard the bad words, they wished they had used better language.

When they were ready to leave, the cook said, "The temperature is the same, but the sun is out. That means we have to worry about frozen shadows. At this temperature the only thing to do is run as fast as you can, maybe that will keep them from freezing." The boys sprinted and when they got to the dorm, they could see their shadows standing 20 feet behind. They ran to get them but the shadows were frozen onto the icy road. That night they built a great bonfire, the gray shadows melted, and the boys decided to only go to camp in the summer. [American Tall Tale]

❧ The Old Man ❧

In the southern part of France, there lived a husband, his wife, and their young son. The husband's father also lived with them, and the wife never stopped complaining about the old man. Among other things, she said, "He makes me sick the way he slurps his soup. It drips off his beard onto his shirt. Why, I'd be ashamed if anyone came to call and saw him."

The husband, wanting peace, asked his father to eat his meal in the other room. But it didn't stop the wife's complaining. She said, "Every time I look up, he is staring at me. He makes me feel like there's something wrong with me. I tell you, either he goes or I go."

The husband didn't want to lose his wife, and he didn't want to lose his father. But his wife refused to change her mind. This put him in the position of having to choose. Finally, he went to his father and said, "Father, it has come to the point that I have to ask you to leave. My wife will not have you in the house any longer."

It was in the middle of Winter, and yet his father only answered, "I understand, son. I will leave."

The thought of having his father go out into the cold was so unbearable to the husband that he asked his little boy to go to the barn and get the horse blanket. He said to his father, "At least the blanket will help to keep you warm."

The little boy went to the barn and returned with a blanket. Obviously, he had cut the blanket in two. The husband was furious. "Why did you cut the blanket in two?" he demanded.

The little boy replied, "Father, I was saving half of it for you and Mother! It will keep you warm when you get old and I have to send you away."

Though it was the custom at that time for grown sons and daughters to put parents out of the house even in the dead of Winter, the boy's words stunned his father. He suddenly realized he was not only going to perform a cruel act, but he was teaching his son to do the same.

He put his hand on the boy's shoulder and said, "Thank you for reminding me of what is right. We don't always have to follow custom." And the boy helped him bring the old man back into the house.

The boy and his father took care of the old man, thereby relieving his wife of the burden. She was able to find some good in him, and didn't wait for the day when he would leave. [Romania]

❦ Androcles and the Lion ❦

Androcles, a Greek slave, ran away from his cruel master and hid in the forest. One day, he came upon a lion. For a moment he froze. He was too frightened to even run. All at once, he saw the lion's paw was bleeding and swollen. Because he was a kind man, Androcles walked closer to the lion. The lion, sensing his kindness, held up its paw and Androcles could see the lion had a thorn in it. Without a word, he very carefully pulled it out. The lion roared as he did it, but didn't bite Androcles. Instead, the lion licked his hand and limped away.

Sometime later, both Androcles and the lion were captured by Roman soldiers. The Roman judges decided to starve the lion for three days and then put it into the arena with Androcles. Everyone for miles around, including the emperor, came to see the hungry lion tear the gentle slave apart. At the appointed time they climbed into their seats and viewed Androcles standing in the arena alone. The trumpets blared, the drums rolled, and the lion was let into the arena. With a roar it went after Androcles. It was ready to spring, when suddenly, he stopped, made a crying sound and lifted its paw towards Androcles. The slave could see where the thorn had been and knew this was his lion. The lion licked his face and hands while the crowds booed. They had wanted a fight.

Well, the judges let Androcles go free after he told them his story. And the lion? It was against all rules but they freed the lion too, and it lived happily in the forest for the rest of its life. [Aesop]

❈ Six Blind Men Sat by the Road ❈

Once upon a road six blind men were led by a young boy to investigate an elephant. The blind men began feeling the elephant to see what it was like.

The first blind man felt the elephant's side, and said, "An elephant is like a wall."

The second blind man felt the elephant's tusks, and said, "No, no, no, the elephant is round and hard."

The third blind man said, as he felt the trunk, "It is very obvious to me that the elephant is round and soft like a snake."

The fourth blind man felt the elephant's leg, and said, "Anyone who knows what his fingers are saying knows that an elephant is like a tree."

The fifth blind man was a big man, and he reached upward and felt the elephant's ears. "No," he said, "an elephant is not like a wall. It is not round and hard. It is not round and soft. It is not like a tree. I have hold of this elephant with my hands and it is like a big fan."

The last blind man laughed and laughed. He had hold of the elephant's tail. "What funny men you are," he said, "and what funny things you say. Only I know what an elephant is like. An elephant is like a rope."

For the rest of their lives the six blind men each believed that the picture they had in their minds of an elephant was correct. [West Africa]

❈ How Wisdom Came to Humans ❈

Anansi, the spider god of the Ashanti people, knew everything. One day, the people offended him and he decided to hide his wisdom away and keep it all for himself. He hid it all in a big pot with a lid. Then he hung that pot around his neck until the pot hit his belly.

He wanted to hang the pot high in a palm tree where no one would find it. However, each time Anansi tried to climb the tree, the pot swung back and forth between him and the tree, which made him lose his balance and fall.

He tried over and over again but always failed to hang the pot in the tree. His son, who had been watching him, said, "Why don't you hang the pot down your back so it is not in your way?"

The suggestion worked so well that Anansi had to admit his son had expressed wisdom. "I thought I had it all in the pot!" he screamed. He was so angry that he threw the pot to the ground, and it broke into many pieces. And that is how wisdom got out of the pot and flew all over the world. [West Africa]

❦ The Talking Mule ❦

Usually, the farmer stayed home on Sunday, but this Sunday he had to go to a funeral. "Put the saddle on Sam," he said to his little boy.

The boy went to the stable, took the saddle off the hook, and said, "Move over, Sam, so I can put this saddle on you."

"For gosh sakes, do I have to work on Sunday?" the mule replied.

The boy quickly ran out of the stable and told his father that the mule had talked. His father said, "For gosh sakes, can't you even saddle a mule?"

"But Sam doesn't want to work on Sunday," said the boy.

The farmer was irritated with his son for telling such a foolish story, so he grabbed the saddle and went out to put it on the mule himself.

"Move over, Sam," he said to the mule.

"You say, 'Move over, Sam,' but you don't bring me anything to eat," said the mule.

The man dropped the bridle and ran. The dog that had followed him to the stall ran, too. "I never heard a mule talk before," said the man.

"Me, neither," said the little dog.

The man ran like the wind into the house and slammed the door. "The mule talked," said the man.

"What?" said his wife.

"I said, 'I never heard a mule talk before.' And the dog said, 'Me, neither.'"

"Ridiculous," said the wife.

"I don't see anything so ridiculous about that," said the cat. "Whoever heard a mule talk?" [United States]

❧ Pancakes ❧

Mouse, Raven, and Snow Ptarmigan* lived in the tundra. One day Mouse called, "Who wants pancakes for supper?"

Raven and Ptarmigan answered enthusiastically, "We do!"

Mouse asked, "Will one of you get me some flour? You'll have to borrow some. I don't have any at all."

"Not me," said Raven, "It's too cold to go out."

"Not me," said Ptarmigan, "I can't find my shoes."

"Then I'll go," said Mouse pleasantly, and she went to the neighbor's to borrow some flour. When she returned, Raven and Ptarmigan were still curled up by the fire. They hadn't moved. She paid no attention to them and filled her biggest bowl with flour, water and fat. Then she called to the lazy ones, "Who'll stir up the batter?"

"Not me," said Raven, "I've been lying on my wing and it hurts."

"Not me," said Ptarmigan, "I want to be close to the fire."

"Then I will," said Mouse, sounding a little irritated. When the batter was smooth, she pleaded, "Won't one of you fry the pancakes? I've done everything else."

"Not me," said Raven, "I don't know how."

"Not me," said Ptarmigan, "I don't want to learn."

"Then I will," said Mouse, in a very angry voice. She fried the pancakes until she had a platter heaped high with them. She set the platter on the table and said very sweetly, "I'm so sorry you don't like pancakes."

"But I do," said Raven, and he leaped up from the fire and ran to the table.

"I don't *like* pancakes, I love them," said Ptarmigan, and knocked over a chair trying to get to the table first.

"Oh, no," said Mouse in her sweetest voice, "You sat and watched while I did all the work. Now you can watch me eat."

Mouse sat down at the table and ate every single pancake on that platter. Every once in a while she would glance at Raven and Ptarmigan. They looked pretty sad, but she didn't feel sorry for them. She only hoped they learned their lesson. [Siberia]

---

* ptarmigan: any of various grouses who live in the far north

❧ Small Talk ❧

Franklin D. Roosevelt, who was the 32nd president of the United States, was a notorious practical joker. Since he had to attend many functions at which he was inevitably introduced to hundreds of strangers, Roosevelt came to realize that most of those he greeted paid little attention to the brief pleasantries that were exchanged.

Roosevelt once put his theory to the test at a party in the White House. As he shook hands with each guest he muttered, "I murdered my grandmother this morning." Only one person responded to this confession: an eminent Wall Street banker. His reply: "She certainly had it coming!"

❧ What'll I Be? ❧

One day, Kainehak, a bear cub, decided he no longer wanted to be a bear. "It would be more fun to be something else," he said, and ran away.

He ran across the tundra   until he found a gopher, who was sitting up and whistling. Kainehak thought, I can do that. He could sit up all right, but he couldn't whistle.

He went on until he found a reindeer. He asked, "Are you good at anything special?"

The reindeer answered, "Well, it happens that I am. I'm a very fast runner."

Kainehak said, "You want to race?" When he didn't win, he said to himself, "Being a reindeer wouldn't be fun."

Next, he saw a duck near a lake. "That looks like fun, just waddling along like that and getting to fly, too. I guess I'll be a duck."

When he asked the duck to teach him to fly, the duck said, "Of course. Follow me." He waddled over to the side of the bluff and took off.

Kainehak followed and fell into the lake. He went under. When he finally surfaced, his arms beat the water hard as he struggled to swim. On shore he shivered and shook from the cold water until he dried off.

When he got home, he didn't tell any stories about his day. He just said, "Hi, Mom! Hi, Dad!" and went to sleep. [Siberia]

❧ Fernando and His Neighbor ❧

Once upon a time, there were two Puerto Rican men who had adjoining farms in the highlands. Fernando was a simple man with gentle manners and a loving heart. His neighbor, Santiago, was very different. He had little patience and a ferocious temper.

One day, as Fernando was gathering fruit, he found three figs hanging on one twig. Fernando called to his wife, "Come see this. I've never seen three figs on one twig. Aren't they beautiful?"

When his wife saw the figs, she agreed. "Yes. They are so beautiful, they are fit for a king."

"You have given me a wonderful idea," said Fernando. "I'm going to bring a basket of figs to our king. I will lay these three on top."

Fernando found a small basket, packed it with the figs, and started his walk to the castle. At the castle he was ushered into the throne room where he gave the figs to the king. The king smiled. "This is my favorite fruit. Where did you get them?"

"I grew them, sir. My wife helped me," Fernando responded. What luck! The king liked figs. Fernando was overjoyed.

The king left the room with the basket of figs. He returned quickly and gave Fernando his basket back ... but filled with gold! He said, "I put your figs in my container and filled your basket with gold because your gift to me was such a thoughtful one. I've always believed a thoughtful man was a good man, and good men should be rewarded."

Fernando couldn't speak. He was overcome. He had always thought of himself as simple Fernando, and because of an act of kindness, the king had rewarded him with gold. He ran all the way home. When he got there, all the neighbors, including Santiago, were waiting to hear about his visit with the king. When he finally got his breath, he said, "We wanted to bring some of our beautiful figs to the king. We didn't know they were his favorite fruit. He was so pleased that he filled my basket with gold."

The neighbors cheered, then danced and sang in celebration, all except Santiago. He went home and filled a cart with figs. The next day he pushed the cart to the castle, demanding an audience with the king. When the gatekeeper refused him admission, Santiago yelled at him so loudly that the king came to see what was going on. The king was a wise man and saw through the peasant's gift. It was not a thoughtful gift, nor an act of sharing. The king did not want any part of it, and he ordered the guard to throw Santiago and his cart out of the castle.

Fernando never told the neighbors why the king gave him the gold. He only whispered it to his wife. Of course, she already knew that her Fernando was a very good man. [Puerto Rico]

FEBRUARY

February

On Groundhog Day you were a queen
Robed in Winter white
With ice-bobs dangling from your ears
And necklace of crystallite.

But now, the days are warming.
Spring rumors have proved true.
Buds are throbbing in the trees.
Roots are stirring, too.

Don't let gray skies detain you.
Put on jeans and shirt.
Freeze your gems for another day.
Go out and flirt with the dirt.

—Pat Nelson

SAVE
the
EARTH

Harry, the Dairy Farmer

Harry is pretty upset because Daisy, his favorite cow, no longer gives sweet milk. It happened like this:

One bitter cold morning Harry went outside to milk the cow, as he always did in the morning. He pulled and pulled and pulled, but couldn't squeeze a drop of milk out of that cow. Suddenly, it dawned on him—he couldn't get milk out of her because her milk bag was frozen! It was one solid chunk. Harry looked at the thermometer. He said, "Why, it's 20 below! No wonder her bag is frozen." Harry quickly found his blowtorch and went to work.

The cow mooed with a feeling of comfort and contentment as the powerful torch's blue flame was applied to the surface of the milk bag. When the milk had partly thawed, Harry went ahead with his milking. And what do you know! That cow gave ice cream!

They say farmers in Canada have been known to keep a fire burning all night under the rear section of their cows during the coldest part of the Winter to prevent the milk from turning into ice cream. [American Tall Tale]

Why the Bear Is Stumpy-Tailed

Long ago, when the world was young, Bear met Fox walking down a path with a string of fish in his mouth that he had just stolen.

"Where did you get those fish, Fox?" Bear asked curiously. He had never seen Fox with fish before.

"Oh, I caught them last night," Fox answered.

"Would you teach me how to catch some fish, Fox?"

"Sure. Why not? You find a rock and take it out onto the frozen pond. Then you pound a hole through the ice with it. When the hole is big enough, sit down with your back to the hole and let that beautiful, long tail of yours hang down in the hole. That's what you catch the fish on. Now, you have to be patient. You can't just leave it there for a few minutes. You want a lot of fish, don't you, Bear?"

"Oh, yes, yes!" Bear was anxious to get on with it.

"Well," drawled Fox, "I guess that's about all there is to it, except be sure to remember to sit long enough. When you think you're ready, stand up and you'll have several fish hanging on your tail."

Bear did what Fox told him to do. He was patient, too. Finally, even Bear's patience wore thin and he decided to pull his tail out of the water. But when he tried to pull it up, it wouldn't come. He turned around and looked, and his tail was frozen in the ice. Bear panicked. With all his strength, he yanked his tail out of the ice, and it broke off.

Ever since then, Bear has been stumpy-tailed. [Russia]

❦ The Man Who Loved to Read ❦

Have you ever been so engrossed in reading a book that your mom called you and you didn't hear her? You weren't trying to put something over on her. You really didn't hear her because your imagination was so busy picturing what you were reading. You were too concentrated to hear. The next time your mother asks why you didn't hear her, just say, "Well, I guess I have the same kind of mind as Abraham Lincoln, the 16th president of the United States."

When Abe was a farm boy, he used to sit and read with his back against the warm chimney in the family's log cabin. Friends of the family would come to call, but they would finally leave because they couldn't get Abe to respond to their conversation. The boy was so focused on what he was reading that he didn't hear them talking to him. They went away thinking that Abe was very strange, which is understandable when you realize that many of these Midwest farmers couldn't read. They thought Abe should be working in the fields. Reading was unimportant to them. For Abe, reading was exciting because it opened up the world.

What did Abe read? He read the Bible and Robinson Crusoe. Aesop's fables were some of his favorites. A friend loaned him *The Life of George Washington* by Parson Weems. He enjoyed the book so much that he took it to work with him to read at lunch. One night, he left his book at the edge of the field where he had been working, and it rained. In the 1800s books were precious possessions in the Midwest because they were so scarce. Because Abe always wanted to be fair, he shucked corn for three days to pay his friend for the ruined book.

Abe Lincoln had many jobs during his lifetime. He was a farmhand, a boat builder, a store clerk, a soldier, a store owner, a postmaster, and a surveyor, but it was reading that brought him to the Congress and the presidency. For years he read law books, walking 20 to 30 miles sometimes to borrow or return them. His reading enabled him to pass the test to receive his law license and opened the door to public office.

Abraham Lincoln was hard-working, honest, and had a wonderful way with words. He not only loved to read, he had a gift for writing. He authored the Gettysburg Address, one of our greatest presidential speeches. He also loved to tell stories to children whenever possible, and to adults, too. No matter what job he held, farmhand or president, Lincoln always used stories to touch the hearts and minds of the people he addressed. For Abraham Lincoln it was the words he read that opened up the world for him.

⊰ Susan B. Anthony ⊱

Susan B. Anthony grew up during a period when women were not considered capable or intelligent enough to control their own lives. When her father's business failed, she saw the creditors take all of her mother's personal belongings. It was as though she didn't even own them.

When Susan was born, there were only three things a girl who wanted to earn a living could do: be a millhand, a servant, or a teacher. Susan became a teacher.

She was paid a dollar-and-a-half per week and was a very successful teacher, even though she was only 17 years old. When she found out the male teachers at the school made four times more than she earned, Susan was angry.

When she gained more experience in life, Susan investigated and found that women could not do what they liked with the property they owned. They couldn't even take care of their own children if anyone objected. And, of course, they weren't allowed in college and did not have the right to vote.

Susan became so angry about this unfairness to American women that she decided to do what she could to change it. Susan B. Anthony became one of the greatest friends women have ever had. Before the close of Miss Anthony's life in 1906, a woman was able to become a doctor, a lawyer, or a businesswoman. Her greatest dream was realized 10 years later. Finally, women were able to vote.

❦ Bad News, Good News ❧

Once, there was a young man walking down a road. When he turned the corner, he was pleased to see an old friend who called out, "Is that you, Bill? I haven't seen you since first grade. How are you?"

Bill answered, "I'm all right, I guess, Jim. I have a girlfriend now."

"Hey, Bill, that's good."

And Bill answered, "Well, it isn't real good, because she always wants to come over to my house."

"Wow!" said Jim, "I'd call that real good. It proves she likes you."

"Well," said Bill, "it's my dog she really likes."

"Gosh, I've never heard of anyone losing out to a dog," Jim replied. "That is bad."

"Well, it is and it isn't, Jim. She brings him dog food."

Jim answered, "Well, she must be a pretty good woman to help you feed him."

And Bill said, "Yes, she is, but she likes the dog next door, too."

"Well, that can be bad if it makes you jealous."

And Bill answered, "It doesn't make me jealous, but the dogs always scrap about it."

"Well," said Jim, "it's terrible to have to put up with dog fights."

"Actually, Jim, I was pretty lucky. A thief came into the neighborhood and robbed every house except mine and my neighbor's. Our dogs were so noisy the thief was afraid to come near."

"Well, that's great, Bill! You didn't lose anything."

"Oh, I lost something all right. My girl ran off with the thief."

And Jim said, "Don't tell me this story has a sad ending."

And Bill smiled for the first time that day, "Oh no, the ending is happy. You see, the thief didn't like dogs around, and so now she comes over to see me."
[American Tall Tale]

❧ The Pot of Cream ❧

As two frogs perched on the edge of a beautiful ceramic pot, they stretched their necks and stuck out their long tongues as far as they could to get a bit of thick cool cream into their mouths and then into their bellies. Eventually, licking the tiny bit of cream became such a task that they decided to stretch their necks even farther hoping to get a whole mouthful of cream at one time. The two frogs stretched their necks to the limit, but lost their balance and fell into the pot.

For a few gleeful moments all they thought about was lapping up the cream. But once they discovered the sides of the pot were slippery and could not be climbed, they knew they were doomed.

The frogs kept swimming in a circle until one of them said desperately, "I can't stand it. There is no way I can get out. I cannot save myself no matter what I do," and he pulled his knees up to his chin, sank to the bottom of the pot, and drowned in the thick sweet cream.

The other frog didn't give up so easily. He kept swimming faster and faster until he could feel the pressure on his body from the cream. When he felt more and more pressure, he realized the cream was becoming thicker and thicker and eventually would become butter. He decided he better get on top of it while he still could.

The frog soon discovered he could swim standing up, and when the cream turned yellow and became firm, the frog simply climbed out of that yellow sea. He jumped to the floor and vowed never again to perch on the edge of a beautiful ceramic pot. Later, the frog realized that his greed to have the cream almost killed him, but his perserverance to climb out of the pot saved his life. [Poland]

❧ The "Babe" ❧

She was 14 years old the first time she read in the newspaper that the Olympics were to be held in Holland that Summer of 1928. Her father saw her reading and smiled. He knew she had the athletic ability to go any place she wanted to go. He could already see that look of determination on her face. She always jutted out her chin when she was deciding to do something. "I'm going to be in the Olympics next year," she said loud enough for her father to hear.

He chuckled, "Babe, you'll have to wait four years. The Olympics don't happen every year."

For a minute, Babe looked crushed, and then she smiled and said with real feeling, "Man, those Olympics are going to be fun. I can hardly wait." And to herself she vowed she was going to become the greatest woman athlete the world had ever seen.

To prepare for the Olympics, she entered the National Track and Field Championships in Illinois. Other athletes competed in teams. Babe was a one-woman team. At the end of the meet, the judge announced, "The Babe Didrikson team won with 30 points. And the first runner-up team, composed of 22 women, had 22 points." What an athlete!

At the 1932 Olympics, Babe set world records in the javelin throw and the 80-meter hurdles. When the champion came home, Grantland Rice, a sports writer, interested her in golf. She went on to win every important women's golf tournament. In 1946 and 1947, she won 17 tournaments in a row.

Babe Didrikson was born with a dream in her pocket. She wanted to be the greatest woman athlete the world had ever seen ... and she succeeded!

❧ The Fox on the Ice ❧

Very early one Winter morning, a fox was drinking at an ice hole and accidentally got his tail wet. When his tail touched the ice, it stuck. It was frozen to the ice!

The fox knew all he had to do to free his tail was to pull very hard on it. However, he was too vain. He knew that if he did this, he would pull all the hair off his tail where it had been stuck to the ice. He wasn't quite ready to mar his beautiful tail and instead decided to wait and see what would happen. Maybe the sun would come out and thaw it.

He waited and waited, but his tail only froze more. He became frightened and frantically ran back and forth. Finally, he saw a wolf step out of the woods and walk toward him. "Wolf! Wolf!" he cried. "Save me! I'm frantic!"

So the wolf stopped and set to work to rescue the fox. Its method was a very simple one: it bit the tail of the fox clean off. So our foolish friend went home tailless, but rejoicing that he was still alive. [Ivan Andreyevich Kriloff]

❦ Brainy Tom ❧

When Tom Edison was only 12 years old, he read a book called the *Decline and Fall of the Roman Empire*. Of course, his mother helped him. Mrs. Edison was a teacher and knew that Tom was a brilliant boy. She could tell because of his excitement at learning anything new. Some doctors thought he had brain trouble because he had such a large head. But his mother knew it was because Tom was smart.

That same year Tom got a job selling fruit, candy, and newspapers on the local express railroad. He was delighted to earn some money and did a good job. But one day the train started without him. When he heard it leaving, he ran toward an open train door. Just about the time he thought he wasn't going to make it, the conductor saw him. He leaned out the door, grabbed Tom by his ears, and pulled him inside the train. Tom felt something snap in his head when the conductor grabbed him. From that day forward, he was deaf.

In his later years, someone asked Edison if it bothered him a great deal to be deaf. His answer was, "It really doesn't bother me because it makes it easier for me to concentrate."

At 15, he became a telegraph operator. The telegraph was a new invention and telegraph offices were opening all over the country. When Tom had extra time, he experimented with the telegraph equipment. This experience enabled him to invent the first voting machine. He also made improvements on the ticker-tape machine. Before long he had become a friend to industry.

With Edison's kind of courage and brilliance, it is not surprising he collected 1,093 patents during his lifetime. When the first phonograph record was played, on the phonograph invented by Tom, it was Tom's voice reciting, "Mary had a little lamb." He invented the first light bulb, motion picture projector, and hundreds of other items.

It might seem that Tom had no time for anything else in his life, but that was not so. He had a wife and three children, and his hobbies included reading and learning about extrasensory perception (ESP)* and other psychic phenomena.**

Thomas Alva Edison, born February 11, 1847, was a brilliant man who spent his life using his creative abilities to improve the world.

---

* extrasensory perception (ESP): residing beyond or outside the ordinary senses

** psychic phenomena: a person apparently sensitive to nonphysical forces

❧ Precious Minutes ❧

Robby Ferrufino awakened every morning with a pocketful of love to share with everyone. That, and his unusual enthusiasm for living, deeply touched the heart of his town, Arvada, Colorado. No one in Arvada will ever forget him.

One January morning in 1987, Robby, a second-grader at Warder Elementary School, was diagnosed as having cancer. By evening, a large tumor had been removed. The family learned chemotherapy would follow.

The drugs made Robby sicker than expected, but he never even complained. He didn't even cry when his prized long brown hair fell out. When he was strong enough, he went back to school wearing a cap on his head. At recess, some bigger, fifth-grade boys thought they'd have fun exposing his baldness. However, before the boys could grab Robby's cap, every second-grader in school came racing across the playground. At first, the big boys were overwhelmed with this smaller army. Later, they were awed by the response of Robby's friends.

By the end of the year, Robby's doctor told the Ferrufino family that Robby was cured. Robby cried amidst family cheers.

"What's wrong, Robby?" his mother asked.

Robby muttered, "I'm crying for all the kids who won't get well."

Robby had it all now: good health, a loving family, and good friends. But late in the year, the cancer returned. The family sobbed, but all Robby asked was, "Will I get to practice for Field Day?" He got his wish, but his health went downhill after that.

If you asked Robby how that year went, he'd say, "Great!" He'd tell you about meeting Mother Teresa, getting a letter from President Bush, making friends with Denver Bronco Karl Mecklenberg, and reading "Happy Birthday, Robby Ferrufino!" on a highway billboard.

All through Robby's illness, he wished that other sick kids could have good times, too. After his death in August 1989, a memorial trust fund was formed to make fun outings available for sick kids and their families. Its aims are to fulfill Robby's wish and ease family strain. The fund also gives a helping hand to non-bilingual Hispanic families with hospitalized children.

In spite of his illness, Robby lived every minute as best he could. In his honor, his school now gives a yearly award to two fifth-graders (one boy and one girl) who give their best during the school year.

After Robby's funeral, Mr. Ferrufino went into his furniture store and found a dove sitting on the cash register. He tried to get it out. It fluttered, then dipped and dived, and came right back. Each time he chased the dove out, it came back. Finally, he guessed this wasn't an ordinary dove. When he brought it home and told his wife the story, she said, "Of course, it's no ordinary dove. This has to be the spirit of our Robby, come home to be with the family."

❦ From Culture to Culture ❧

Sometimes different cultures tell the same story with a different setting but similar characters. Remember when something fell on Henny Penny's head and she told all her friends the sky was falling and they all set out to tell the king? The people of India have a story about a nervous little rabbit who heard a big thump when she walked under a coconut palm tree. She didn't know what fell, but the sound made her shudder until she cried, "The earth is falling in!" and ran away as fast as she could.

She soon met another rabbit who wanted to know where she was going in such a hurry. The little rabbit didn't stop running, but looked back and cried, "The earth is falling in! I'm running away!" Now there were two rabbits running. When they met another rabbit, the second rabbit told the third, and the third rabbit told the fourth, and on and on, all shouting, "The earth is falling in!" as they chased each other.

When the bigger animals of the forest heard the shouting, they investigated and quickly joined the shouting runners. There was a deer, a camel, a tiger, an elephant, some sheep, a wild boar, and a lion. Not until the lion roared so loudly that palm branches quivered did the animals stop running and shouting. Once they were quieted, the lion walked down the line asking each one, "How do you know the earth is falling in?" Each animal had to admit to getting the information from another animal. When it was the nervous little rabbit's turn to speak, she looked up at that big lion and said, "I saw it."

"Where?" asked the lion.

"Over by that tree," said the rabbit, and pointed to it.

The little rabbit was too frightened to walk over to the tree, so the lion carried her to it on his back. As soon as they got there, a great big coconut fell off the tree onto the hard ground and made a big thump. The little rabbit could hardly speak, she was so surprised. In a whisper she said to lion, "It sounded like that coconut sounded, not like the earth is falling in."

"Jump down!" said the lion. "I want you to learn something from this experience. The next time you hear something that scares you, don't run. Stop and look closely. Don't guess. You'll be surprised to find out how many noises you've run away from because you didn't stop to figure out what you really heard and what you imagined you heard.

The English, Scandinavians, Chinese and Tibetans all tell a similar tale. Since the story is very old, one wonders how it happened in a pre-electric world that so many cultures could have similar stories.

⚜ Shoes Don't Match ⚜

One day a very high Chinese official couldn't understand why he was so uncomfortable walking. Actually, he was limping. But he was not a lame man. When he stopped and looked at his feet, he saw what was the matter. His shoes didn't match! He had a boot with a high heel on one, and on the other was a shiny black shoe.

He said to his servant, "Look what I have done. I've put on shoes that don't match. Would you please go home and hurry back with the right shoes?"

The servant did as he was asked, but in a few minutes was back without a shoe. He said, "It's no use to change your shoes. The pair at home is just like these." [China]

⚜ Doing the Right Thing ⚜

A long time ago four young lawyers on horseback trotted down a narrow path on their way to town. Occasionally they could see bright green sprouts pushing through the wet, black earth. But mostly the road was lined with slimy mud.

As they passed through a grove of trees, one behind the other, they heard a great fluttering in the branches over their heads. "Cheep," cried a baby robin trapped on an island of green grass. The riders stopped for a moment. When the lawyer on the first horse realized the situation, he was quick to say, "Well, come on now. Don't go gettin' soft on me. We don't have time to rescue a bird. We need to get to town for our meeting. Let's go!" he demanded, and he swatted his horse and galloped off.

The next two riders looked yearningly at the baby robin ... and then at all that mud. They, too, turned their horses toward town. Later, when they realized the fourth rider was not with them, they figured he was probably trying to rescue that bird. What a laugh they had at his oversensitivity.

The fourth lawyer got off his horse and struggled through the mire to the baby robin. Then, with one arm free, he managed to climb the tree and return the baby to its nest, in spite of the parent birds dive-bombing him. When he finally got down, his shoes and pants were covered with mud. He was late to his meeting and laughed at by his lawyer friends.

That wasn't the first time, or the last time, that the fourth lawyer did what he thought was right in spite of everything that stood in his way. That fourth lawyer was Abraham Lincoln, the 16th president of the United States, born February 12, 1809.

❦ The Wolf and the Dog ❦

A lean, hungry wolf and a plump, well-fed watchdog met one night in the woods. After the usual greetings, the wolf said, "How fat and sleek you look. Tell me, how do you manage to live so well?"

"You might live as well, if you did as I do," replied the watchdog.

"How is that?" asked the wolf.

"I watch the house and keep away the thieves," the dog said.

"That doesn't seem too hard. I'm sure I could do a good job, and it would be such a relief not to worry about a warm roof over my head." The wolf was becoming enthusiastic about the idea.

The wolf and the dog continued discussing the differences in their two lives until the wolf noticed a mark around the dog's neck. "What's that?" he asked the dog.

"It's nothing to speak of," said the dog. "Probably the collar by which I'm tied sometimes."

"What?" asked the wolf, "You mean you can't always go where you please?"

"Well, as you probably know, I am looked upon as a pretty fierce fellow, so they tie me in the daytime. At night I roam about. The day isn't bad. The children and servants treat me well, and I have plenty to eat." Suddenly, the dog said, "Where are you going? I thought we were going to become better friends."

And the wolf replied, "I'm going to my cold home under a porch, and I hope I find something to eat on the way. You may have a fine life, but I would rather live on an old crust of bread and remain free than live like a prince and wear chains around my neck." [Aesop]

⚛ George Washington ⚛

On George Washington's sixth birthday he was given a fine hatchet. Like most boys, he was extremely proud of it, and he spent his time chopping everything that got in his way. He especially enjoyed entering his mother's garden to hack the stakes she used to support her peas. One day in the garden, he came upon a beautiful little cherry tree. Because it was in his way, he just chopped it down.

The next morning his father went for a walk through the garden. When he came upon his lovely little cherry tree lying on its side with its leaves already shrivelling, he was furious. He was certain George had done it and hurried to find him.

By this time, George realized he had done something that was bound to make his father angry. He was so scared that he ran to his room and waited. He had just shut the door when his father came bursting into the room. He grabbed George by the shoulders and said, "Do you know what happened to my dear little cherry tree?"

George rubbed the tears out of his eyes with the back of his hand and said, "I'm sorry, Papa. I did it. I don't know why I did it. I just did." Then came a flood of tears.

Suddenly, George's father was so touched by the honesty of his young son that he took George in his arms and said, "I'm so proud of you. I can plant another cherry tree. That's no problem. Don't worry about it. What's important here is that I have found out that I have a very honest son. I will never forget this day." And I doubt that George did, either.

❧ Why Bear Sleeps All Winter ❧

A very long time ago, when animals could talk, Bear ruled the forest. All of the animals worked for him, and he was not a good boss. They all grew to hate him, but they couldn't do anything about it. He was too big and they were too afraid. The only time they had any peace was when Bear slept.

One night, Bear fell asleep in a hollow tree, and Rabbit thought that if all the animals brought enough twigs and rocks, they could fill the opening of the tree so Bear couldn't get out. The animals busied themselves and carried out Rabbit's plan. And it worked! Bear slept on and on. Each time he awakened, he saw only darkness. So, he thought it was still night and fell asleep again.

The animals spent a wonderful winter without Bear. When six weeks had passed and he still hadn't gotten up, the animals figured they were rid of him forever. One day, in the Spring, when they were playing in the woods, they said, "Old Bossy Bear must be dead by this time. Let's pull away the rocks and twigs."

But when the light shined into the hollow tree, Bear awakened. He stretched and yawned, stood, and said, "Oh, I had such a good sleep. Well, look at that, there are buds on the trees. I must have slept all Winter. Best Winter I ever spent."

The animals were sorry to see him back, but hoped the long sleep would help Bear to be a kind boss. Then, bear vowed he would sleep all Winter every year, so they did have something to look forward to. [Native American]

❧ Red Dan, the Flying Farmer ❧

It was the middle of Winter and Red Dan got up as usual to do the farm chores. He heard a commotion on the pond near the barn and was astonished to find a flock of wild geese with their feet frozen in the ice. They were honking loudly enough to wake the dead! With visions of roast goose running through his head, Red Dan picked up an old spoke of a wagonwheel, rushed onto the ice, and began swinging at the geese.

An old gander, the leader of the flock, gave a loud, commanding "honk." As one, the geese flapped their wings and rose into the air, carrying the cake of ice and Red Dan along with them. Up and up they went, sailing through the sky like an airplane, with Red Dan on the ice cake among the flapping wings.

He was worried. Those geese were headed south, and Red Dan knew that when they reached the tropics the cake of ice would melt, and he would fall to the ground as the geese flew happily away.

Knowing that something had to be done, Red Dan got busy again with that old wagonwheel spoke. He punched a hole through the ice, freed several of the geese, and then grabbed onto their legs. He dropped through the hole using the birds as a parachute and floated safely to Earth.

He received an awful bump from the landing, but he still held onto the geese. A neighbor picked him up, and Dan took the neighbor home to fix him roast goose for breakfast. [American Tall Tale]

⚜ The Folklorist ⚜

A folklorist is someone who gathers the stories of the people—the stories the people *tell* each other, not the stories that are printed. Most folklorists collect very old tales. The familiar stories of "The Three Bears" and "The Three Little Pigs" were collected about 200 years ago.

Even today we tell stories. Some of these are repeated over and over again. If a folklorist finds them, he or she will call them urban, modern, or belief legends. These stories are usually kind of spooky and sometimes funny.

One of the stories often told around boy scout campfires is "The Golden Arm." It is called a "jump tale" because at the end, the storyteller jumps at his or her listeners. Other "jump tales" include "The Big Toe" and "Give Me Back My Liver."

A classic spooky tale is "The Vanishing Hitchhiker." The story has several versions and one goes like this: One night a young couple was driving home when they saw a young girl hitchhiking. They stopped and picked her up. She climbed into the back seat and told them where she lived, then became very quiet. The couple became involved with their own conversation, and when they came to what looked like the house the girl had directed them to, they turned around thinking she was probably asleep, but she wasn't there at all. The couple decided to knock on the door and tell the people what had happened. Imagine their shock when they described the girl they had picked up and the woman who answered the door said, "Yes, that's my daughter. I expected her because it is her birthday. She was struck by a hit and run driver many years ago. She tends to come back on her birthday. I've never seen her, but people like you come and tell me about her."

If you liked that urban legend, you will also enjoy reading some of Jan Harold Brunvand's books about urban legends. They are *The Vanishing Hitchhiker*, *The Choking Doberman*, and *Curses! Broiled Again!* Though they are shelved in adult nonfiction, librarians might be willing to check them out to kids.

MARCH

March

March tiptoes
Through the snow
In high heels.
North and south winds
Argue over her future.

—Pat Nelson

❧ Tom, Dick, and Harry ❧

When Jack was a kid, it never bothered him that he had no brothers or sisters. He thought there were many advantages to being an only child. Sharing wasn't a big problem, so it was never difficult to keep track of his possessions. He had to admit that sometimes it was a little lonely, but Jack's mom was good about letting him have a friend over for the night.

As Jack grew older, he realized that brothers and sisters, without knowing, teach each other to stand up for themselves. They didn't let other kids take advantage of them like he did. He never suspected anyone would lie to him, and he couldn't take teasing at all. He had to learn these things when he was an adult.

Jack married, and soon he and his wife had three sons, Tom, Dick, and Harry. The boys were happy and healthy, but if a fight happened, Jack would help them resolve it. In this way he hoped that he was helping his sons to become better adults.

Jack expected that when the boys reached high school, they would be able to stand up for themselves without knocking someone down. But that isn't what happened. As years passed, the fighting became worse instead of better. Any little disagreement grew into a boxing match. Jack knew he needed to stop this, but he wasn't sure how to do it.

One day, after a big three-way fight, Jack called his sons outside. He was standing in the yard holding a bundle of sticks. There must have been 10 or 15 quarter-inch sticks about 2 feet long. Jack handed the bundle to each boy and asked him to break it. Each boy tried and failed. Finally, Dick, sounding rather bored, asked, "Dad, what's this all about?"

Jack said, "You'll see." He held the bundle up and instructed each boy to pull out a stick. When each had one in his hand, Jack said, "All right, now try to break this one stick in the same way you tried to break the bundle of sticks."

Tom, Dick, and Harry had no trouble breaking their sticks. They all thought the whole thing was a bit strange. Tom said, "I don't get it."

And Dick chimed in, "I don't either."

Jack put his arms around all three of them. "Guys, what I am trying to tell you is this. I want you to remember that you're Tom, Dick, and Harry, all with the same last name. You're brothers! Single sticks and boys alone are easily broken, but if you stay together and remember you are brothers, no one can defeat you.

While Jack's lesson didn't work forever, it worked long enough for Tom, Dick, and Harry to learn to be persuasive with their tongues rather than their fists. They also grew to appreciate each other and their father. [Aesop]

❦ Johnny Appleseed ❦

Some people carry little dreams around in their heads, such as something they dream of owning or a vacation they want to take. Some carry big dreams, such as a career as a professional or a score they want to beat. And then there are some people who carry strange dreams in their heads and are compelled to spend their lives making those dreams come true.

Johnny Appleseed had a strange dream. He loved apples, and he thought their blossoms were the most beautiful in the world. Pioneers were moving into the Middle West. Johnny thought they needed something to make the land more beautiful and more productive. And, of course, he thought of apples. He tramped through Pennsylvania, Ohio, and Indiana whistling a tune as he handed out packages of seed. When the settlers let him, he would plant a whole orchard for them and then stop back now and then to check on its progress. He planted seeds along the rivers and in the meadows. When settlers tried to pay him, he wouldn't take a penny. It seemed to Johnny that accepting money would take the value away from his dream.

People laughed at him when he wouldn't take money. They laughed even harder when they found out he wouldn't eat meat. "I just couldn't kill an animal," he'd say. And he didn't, not even mosquitoes.

Johnny Appleseed lived in poverty and was ridiculed. Yet, some people hailed him as a hero and a saint. [United States]

❦ Little Moron Tale ❦

Two morons were painting a house. The one on the ground asked the one on the ladder, "Have you a good hold on your brush?"

"Yes, why?"

"Because I am going to take away the ladder," replied the first.

Later that day, one of them was hanging out an upper story window when he called to the other on the ground. "How can I get down?"

The second answered, "I'll turn on my flashlight and you can slide down the beam."

"Nothing doing," said the first. "When I get about halfway down, you'd turn it off." [United States]

❧ A Strange Tidal Wave ❧

In 1919 there was a terrible explosion in the city of Boston. It was a rather warm Winter day when, suddenly, there was a terrible rumbling, loud enough to make one's hair stand on end. An eyewitness reported, "It was like a thousand machine guns."

In what seemed like just moments, a terrifying tidal wave rode through the city with such force that loaded freight cars were tossed like matchboxes. Beams of wood and sheets of steel were hurled through the air. A team of horses was slammed through a fence, and everywhere people were running and screaming. Just as terror had struck the people of ancient Pompeii, fleeing from the lava of Vesuvius, citizens of North Boston dashed on foot, drove horse carriages and automobiles, and even rode bicycles as they tried to escape the onrushing tidal wave. But few succeeded. They were swallowed up instead. In minutes it was over. What had once been a place where children played, people walked, and workers labored was now a scene of death and destruction.

Today, we are able to predict disasters. However, no one in Boston could have ever predicted the 1919 explosion at the Purity Distilling Company that resulted in a tidal wave of 2.3 million gallons ... of molasses!

❧ Puzzling Questions ❧

Riddles have always been popular. These little puzzling questions are fascinating to both old and young. Ask your grandmother about riddles. You might be surprised how many she knows.

Even people of ancient times loved riddles. You can find them in the Bible in the book of Solomon and the book of Judges. The Greeks loved them and took them seriously. It is said that Homer, one of their greatest poets, died trying to guess the answer to a riddle. The Greeks say that the Sphinx killed men because they could not answer the following question: What is that which has 4 feet in the morning, 2 feet at noon, and 3 feet at night? The answer: Man. As a baby he creeps on his hands and knees, in mid-life he walks on 2 feet, and in old age he totters along with the aid of a cane, or a "third leg."

"Amusing Questions" is a very old riddle book that was written during the Middle Ages. It's a good thing the book includes the answers, because no one today could correctly guess such a riddle as: What is that that never was, or never will be? The answer: A mouse's nest in a cat's ear.

Well, everything changes—even riddles. You'll probably be able to answer these questions: What's black and white and red all over? No, it's not a newspaper, it's an embarrassed zebra. How about trying one more? When is a door not a door? The answer is: When it's ajar.

Have a good time with riddles. You might even try making up your own.

Spring Equinox

The old Indian known as Ice Man sat in his tepee huddled close to his dying fire. His long, white hair hung loosely around him like a silken shawl.

As he looked outside, he felt contented to see the land was still white and becoming whiter with fresh falling snow. Suddenly, he saw someone coming up the hill. It was that boy with the big, rosy cheeks, and pants that didn't cover his knees. As the figure came closer, he could see it was not really a boy, but a beautiful young man. A wreath of sweetgrass was tied around his head, and in his hand he carried a small bunch of wildflowers.

Ice Man called to him, "Come in. Come in. I have only a bit of fire left, but it might be enough to warm you." The young man stepped inside the tepee and warmed his hands over the few orange coals. Ice Man asked, "Why are you here? It is still cold."

"I bring you a message of what will come," answered the young man.

"Well, then," said Ice Man, who was not ready to give up his power, "I will tell you of the wonders I perform." The old man pulled a beautifully carved pipe out of his bag. He filled it with good-smelling, dried leaves and lit it from the last coals of the fire. He puffed a little and then blew the smoke into the four directions—North, South, East, and West. He then gave the pipe to the young man who smoked it as Ice Man had.

After the pipe ceremony, Ice Man said with as much strength as he could, "When I blow my breath, still water becomes hard and so clear, I can see my face in it."

Not to be outdone, the young man spoke up quickly, "I only have to breathe and the forests become a carpet of wildflowers."

Ice Man assured this young fellow that old men know how to brag, too. "When I shake my long hair, snow covers everything and leaves turn brown and fall to the ground. My breath blows them away." The old man looked outside to gaze at his handiwork, only to find the snow had stopped falling and the sun was now shining. At this moment Ice Man knew his time had ended. He said to the young man, "I am proud of my power to bring Winter, but when the birds fly to warmer places and the animals run to hide, I am sad and lonely."

The young man understood and said quietly, "When I shake my hair, soft rain falls and plants stretch towards the sky. My breath melts the ice, and when I sing, the birds fly back from the south."

Ice Man didn't answer as he was lost in his thoughts. Then he heard the song of a robin on the top of his tepee, and the trickle of melting ice in the creek. When he saw his fire was almost out, tears rolled down Ice Man's face.

As the sun rose higher and higher in the sky, the tepee became warmer and warmer, and Ice Man became smaller and smaller. When the last orange ember turned black, a small white and pink flower bloomed where the fire had burned. The flower came to be known as wild portulaca and its bloom means Spring has arrived. [Native American]

❦ Wonderful Brain and Nerve Tonic ❧

John Pemberton was a pharmacist who loved to make home remedies. He cooked his tonics and medicines in a three-legged pot behind his drugstore. In the 1880s this was the way most pharmacists worked.

One day John found a new recipe using the African kola nut and coca leaves. He cooked it, but found it tasted very bitter. To sweeten it, he added sugar and a blend of caramel, lime, nutmeg, cinnamon, and vanilla. When it cooled, he tasted it and found it was much better.

John took some of his new concoction to a friend and asked him to mix them a drink of one part of John's syrup to five parts water. It was great! But he wanted to make it better. When they tried soda water instead of plain tap water, both men screamed, "Delicious!"

John sold his new drink as a nerve and tonic stimulant, but it didn't sell. He tried advertising. A big, colorful advertisement called it a "Wonderful Brain and Nerve Tonic." It still didn't sell. Then he named his product Coca-Cola—but it still didn't sell.

John Pemberton was so disappointed that he sold his interest in Coca-Cola for $1,750. The company changed owners several times until Mr. Asa Candler bought it in 1888 and advertised Coca-Cola only as a soft drink, not as a medicine. By 1895 you could buy "Coke" in every state and territory of the United States. Today, Coca-Cola sells 560 million drinks each day.

❦ The Lunar Eclipse ❧

One day when Moon was under an eclipse, she complained to Sun, "My dearest friend, what is happening? Are you angry? Why do you not shine upon me as you used to do?"

"I didn't know I wasn't shining upon you, Moon. I'm surprised. I certainly did not intend to slight you."

"Oh, no," said Moon after more careful observation. "Now I see the reason. It isn't your fault at all. I see that dirty planet, the Earth, has got between us." [Robert Dodsley]

❦ The King and the Bees ❧

One day King Solomon was sitting on his throne, when suddenly, the door to the throne room was opened and the Queen of Sheba walked in carrying two identical bouquets.

"O King," she said, "in my own country, so far away, I have heard a lot about your power and glory, but much more about your wisdom. Men have told me that there is no riddle so clever that you cannot solve it. Is this true?"

"Yes, it is true," answered King Solomon, but all the time wondering why the Queen of Sheba had come to his court.

"Well, I have a puzzle that I would like to show you," said the queen. She held in each hand a beautiful bouquet of flowers. The bouquets were so alike she could hardly tell the difference between them. "One of these bouquets," said the queen, "is made of flowers plucked from your garden. The other is made from artificial flowers, shaped and colored by a skillful craftsman. All I want you to do is tell me which bouquet is real."

The king looked puzzled. Both bouquets looked real to him. When he moved uneasily on his throne, one of his advisors came over and whispered in his ear, "It is a trick, sir. They are too identical. They both have to be real."

"Look at the flowers carefully," instructed the queen, "then give me your answer."

Solomon looked at the bouquets from every side. He frowned. He stroked his chin, then bit his lips, but he did not answer.

Suddenly, the king remembered that close to his window was a climbing vine filled with beautiful sweet flowers. Just that morning he had seen many bees flying among these flowers and gathering honey from them.

"Open the window," he said to his servant boy, and the boy obeyed. The queen was standing quite near with the two bouquets still in her hands.

Two bees immediately flew through the window. And soon there was another and another. All flew to the flowers in the queen's right hand. Not one of the bees flew to the flowers in her other hand.

Solomon smiled and turned to the queen, "I do believe, Queen, the bees have given you my answer."

And the queen said, "You are wise, King Solomon. You gather knowledge from the little things which pass by common men unnoticed.

King Solomon lived 3,000 years ago. He built a great temple in Jerusalem, and was famous for his wisdom. [Israel]

⚜ The Magic Purse ⚜

Most Irishmen know about the red, silk magic purse that a leprechaun always carries. It has a delightful magic about it: Whenever it is emptied, it refills by itself.

Mike O'Hara knew about a leprechaun's magic purse. That's why, when he saw a leprechaun lurking in the woods, he slipped behind the leprechaun, grabbed him, and frisked him. It was Mike's lucky day! There was the purse with a coin inside.

Mike was rich now. As soon as he spent the coin, the purse would refill. However, he became so excited about the idea that he would soon have all the money he wanted that he became lazy. Instead of going to his job, Mike decided to go to Mrs. McCarthy's Cafe and treat everyone to a cup of coffee.

Mrs. McCarthy, the owner, said, "I'll pour the coffee if you'll pay me today. No more credit, Mike O'Hara!" She poured the coffee. Mike, proud as a peacock, took the coin out of the purse and closed it. With great expectation, he reopened it. But the purse did not refill. He tried again and again, but every time he opened it, the purse was empty!

Mike didn't really know how tricky leprechauns are. If he had, he would have figured that they carry two purses similar in appearance, but only one was magic. Mike had been tricked, and he was very angry about it. Imagine being tricked by a silly leprechaun! Not only that, he was going to have to pay Mrs. McCarthy for all that coffee she served to his friends!

Months later, when Mrs. McCarthy's bill was finally paid, Mike decided to never fool around with leprechauns again. [Ireland]

❦ Testing the Water ❧

About 20 years ago the Pennington, New Jersey, environmental commission decided that it had become too expensive to hire professional technicians to test the purity of the streams in its valley. The commissioners asked Kay Widmer, a high school science teacher, to teach her students to do the testing. Kay knew the valley well. She had trampled the hills and waded the streams in that area all of her life. She knew her science well, too, and saw the request as a great teaching opportunity.

In the beginning, the students looked forward to the project like they would a holiday, but when they became used to the new outdoor classroom, they forgot about play. Water became a very interesting subject. The students trapped several kinds of insects in the water, to which they turned up their noses. Their teacher explained that the insects were good bugs, the kind that killed bad bugs. They soon began thinking of mayflies*, waterbeetles**, stoneflies***, and caddis fly larvae**** as their partners in keeping the streams clean.

As the students became more experienced, they learned to use chemicals to measure the amount of pollution in the streams. And when they found too much ammonia and nitrates in the water, they became detectives, prowling the valley until they discovered the source of the pollution. Sometimes it was serious enough to contact the health department. The students involved in these searches felt as if they were doing something that mattered to the people who lived in the valley.

Kay Widmer still teaches her outdoor science class. Some of her students have become environmental scientists, lawyers, and technicians, and all of her students have become better-informed citizens because of a dedicated teacher.

---

*   mayflies: live only a day because they do not eat; they dance, mate, and lay their eggs in streams and ponds

**   waterbeetles: live in freshwater ponds and streams and capture and eat almost all small pond dwellers

***   stoneflies: live as larvae attached to stones in creek bottoms

**** caddis fly larvae: live as worms in a tube of sand and sticks in streams and brooks

❦ Beauty Business ❧

Sarah's hair was falling out. Frantically, she tried every medicine she could find, but nothing worked. Thoughts of buying a wig worried her to death because she didn't have any money. She was a 20-year-old widow with a baby girl.

In her frenzy one night, she dreamed she told an old man about her hair problem, and he gave her a formula for a scalp medicine. The dream was so real to her that she mixed the formula and put it on her scalp. In a few weeks she could see a difference. Her hair was growing in!

Sarah stopped worrying and started working. If the formula grew new hair for her so quickly, why wouldn't it work on others? She mixed the formula again, bottled it, and sold it. She became quite successful and dreamed of having her own beauty products business. In five years, she had a company that earned $7,000 a week and employed 5,000 salesladies. She married C. J. Walker, a newspaperman. Now she was in a position to dream again. And she did!

As Madame C. J. Walker, Sarah dreamed of awarding prizes to the 5,000 black women who worked for her, but not for the highest sales of beauty products. She wanted to award prizes to those who gave the most community service to the black community after hours.

Madame C. J. Walker, determined, energetic, and a real dreamer, became the United States' first black female millionaire.

⅋ A Trip to the Sky ⅋

A little pea slipped under a house and began to grow. It grew as high as the floor of the house, and one day the old man who lived there heard the pea knocking on the floor. He cut a hole in the floor, and when he saw the pea, he watered it. It grew and grew until he had to cut a hole in the ceiling for it to grow through. The pea grew through the attic, and the man cut a hole in the roof. It grew through the roof until it reached the sky.

The man said to his wife, "Goodbye." I'm going to climb to the sky and see what that pea is doing." He climbed and climbed and climbed until he reached a big house that was empty except for some food on the stove. It smelled so good that he sat right down to eat, when a goat with seven eyes began staring at him.

The man called out, "Sleep, little eye! Sleep, little eye!" And one eye closed. Then he did the same thing five more times. He didn't see the seventh eye because it was in the back of the goat's head. When he thought the goat couldn't see him, he ate all the food and stretched out and went to sleep.

When the owner of the big house came home, the goat told the man what he had seen with his seventh eye. The man called his servants to throw the intruder out. The poor, sleepy man ran to where the pea vine was growing, but he couldn't find it, so he looked around until he found some cobwebs. He grabbed the cobwebs and twisted them into a rope. Then he fastened the rope on the sky and slid down, but the rope wasn't long enough! The man fell and landed in a swamp, where he got stuck in the mud. When a duck flew by, he grabbed her tail and she pulled him out of the mud.

The point: Those who climb ropes to the sky would be better off if they learned how to fly. [Russia]

APRIL

April

Hooray! It's Spring!
I wouldn't do anything
To stop it
Or change it
In any way!
I guess that's all
I have to say,
Except . . .
Hooray! It's Spring!

— Pat Nelson

❧ Watch Out! It's April Fools' Day! ❧

It's here again, that crazy day when everyone's desire is to make a fool of someone, or to prevent someone from making a fool of him or her. The custom of playing tricks on April Fools' Day is so old its origins have been lost. And yet, year after year, people are still playing tricks and getting tricks played on them.

Many people play the same kinds of tricks year after year. They have fun pouring sugar in the salt shaker or serving an empty egg shell in a fancy egg cup or even taping a note on someone's back that says "Kick me!" Everyone seems to have a good time in spite of a bit of embarrassment on the part of the victim.

There are others who think only of bigger and better April Fools' tricks. In London on April 1, 1860, a particularly creative individual sent out many beautiful invitations for the annual ceremony of Washing the White Lions at the Tower of London, a well-known site in the center of the city. Those invited were directed to go through a white gate at 2:00 p.m. Of course, there wasn't any ceremony. And many horse-drawn carriages rattled around the Tower of London spending hours looking for a nonexistent white gate. Londoners didn't want to admit they had been fooled. It was too embarrassing. However, the practical jokers had a wonderful time and spurred on by their success, were already thinking about April 1, 1861.

The first day of April has been celebrated all over the world. If someone pulls a trick on you in France on this day, you are called an April fish, or "poisson d'Avril." In Scotland, the victim of the April joke is called a gowk, or a cuckoo.

Sometimes it doesn't pay to be too suspicious on April Fools' Day. Many years ago prominent citizens in France, seeing the notorious Duke of Lorraine climbing over the prison wall, ran to tell the guards. But because it was April Fools' Day, the guards were ready for pranksters. They just laughed. "You can't fool us," the guards said. "We know your kind." And the famous Duke of Lorraine escaped.

François Rabelais, a great writer of humor, managed to get some free transportation because it was April 1. He was living in France and wanted to travel to Paris, the capital, but he didn't have any money. So, he filled some empty bottles with water and marked the containers, "Poison for the Royal Family of France." As Rabelais had planned, police saw him with the bottles and within minutes they hustled him into a carriage and had their fastest horses take him to the prison in Paris. It was a free ride, and a swift one, and once there Rabelais managed to escape.

Most of us don't create such involved tricks for April Fools' Day. We're content with glueing a quarter to the sidewalk, or tying a string to a purse, hiding, and when someone tries to pick it up, pulling it away. But you never know what we might think up for next year.

❧ Why the Baby Deer Wears Spots ❧

Years ago, when the spirits still roamed the Earth, one of them happened to be sitting by a fire recounting the good deeds he had done for the many creatures he knew.

"I have helped almost every creature," he said. "I have made feathers for the birds so they may flock together and flee from their enemies. I gave the porcupine his quills, the buffalo his horns, the wolf his strong teeth, and the deer and the rabbit their speed. In fact, nearly every creature has received from me some form of defense to use whenever he is in need." The Spirit soon realized his error, however, when a mother deer sped to his side, closely followed by her fawn, or baby deer.

"Oh, Spirit," she said, "you gave to me my speed, and to others you have given some means of protection, but how is such a young one to keep away from enemies?"

"I will take care of that," replied the Spirit. "I shall make him so hard to see that he will be safe while hiding, and no animal shall ever find him by his smell."

So, taking his brush and paints, the Spirit carefully painted spots upon the fawn's body until he blended with the shadows in the grass and brush.

From then on the mother deer found that she could eat while the fawn hid, and though the spots disappeared when the fawn was full grown, he no longer needed them, for then the gift of speed protected him. [Native American]

❧ How the Moon and Stars Came to Be ❧

Long ago, when the sky rested very close to the Earth, there was a beautiful young woman who took her mortar* and pestle** down to the beach to pound her rice. Before she started, she removed the lovely necklace she wore and the ornamental comb that held up her hair. She looked for a place to put them while she worked, but finally she just hung them on the sky above her head.

As she pounded her rice, each time she raised her pestle in the air it struck the sky. She hit the sky so many times it began to rise. Amazed, she watched the sky rise and her ornaments with it. Higher and higher the sky rose until she knew her beloved comb and necklace were lost forever, for the sky lifted higher than she or any human could reach.

However, when night came, she gazed in wonder at the sky and saw that her shining comb had become the moon and the beads of her necklace had become bright stars that all the world could enjoy. And the sky never hung low again. [Mindanao]

---

* mortar: a strong container used for pounding substances

** pestle: club-shaped tool for pounding in a mortar

❧ The Ride of Paul Revere ❧

In 1775, Boston was filled with British soldiers, whom the people knew had been sent by the king of England to suppress them. Everyone had been watching Boston for days. If a war began in the colonies, it was expected to happen in Boston. Paul Revere was one of the many who was watching for trouble.

One day a friend of Paul's secretly told him that the king's soldiers were going to Concord (a town about 30 miles away) to seize gunpowder for their guns. Paul was not surprised nor was he hesitant to act. "We cannot let this happen," he said. "I can ride from here to Concord and alert the farmers, but you must help me."

"Just tell me what to do," said his friend.

"Return to Boston and watch. As soon as the soldiers are ready to go, hang a lantern in the old North Church if they're coming by land. If you see they are coming across the river, hang two. As soon as I get your message, I will mount my horse and ride to Concord to awaken everyone."

That night Paul stood by his horse as he watched and waited. Ten o'clock and he saw nothing but the dim form of the old North Church in the light of the moon. The clock struck eleven, still no lanterns. Suddenly, a light flashed from the church. The soldiers had started. Paul put his foot in the stirrup. He was ready to mount when another light flashed, telling him the soldiers would come across the river.

Paul Revere sprang into his saddle and away he rode through villages and farmland shouting, "Up! Up! The soldiers are coming. Defend yourselves!" By the time the farmers reached their windows, they couldn't see Paul. He was too far away. But they could still hear his voice and his horse's hooves.

The alarms spread quickly, as quickly as though a fire were raging. Sleepy farmers put on their clothes and lined the roads to the surprise of the British soldiers. There were skirmishes along the way and when the king's men got to Concord, they burned down the courthouse. There was also a battle at Lexington, a town nearby. The Revolutionary War, the war to preserve our freedom, had begun.

Paul Revere's ride is a well-remembered event in American history, not because of its great importance, but because Henry Wadsworth Longfellow dramatized it so well in his poem *Paul Revere's Ride*. It is a very long poem, but I thought you might enjoy just the first verse.

Paul Revere's Ride
_____

> Listen, my children, and you shall hear
> Of the midnight ride of Paul Revere,
> On the eighteenth of April, in seventy-five;
> Hardly a man is now alive
> Who remembers that famous day and year.

❧ The Lullaby ☙

It was Spring and two snow buntings* returned to the cliffs of the Bering Strait from the south. They built a nest on a high crag at the edge of the sea. They soon had a baby son who cried all the time. To quiet him, Mother Bunting sang him a song.

Raven heard it and thought it was the most beautiful song he had ever heard. "Mother Bunting, give me your song," Raven begged.

"No, Raven, I need it for putting my baby to sleep," the mother answered.

Angrily, Raven said, "If you don't give me that song, I'll snatch it from him."

When Mother Bunting answered, "Oh, no, you won't," Raven swooped down and snatched the song.

Father Bunting heard the baby's cries and flew back to the nest. When he heard what the Raven had done, he was furious. "I'm going to find that thief and snatch the song from his throat!" He flew until he found Raven. Father Bunting knew he had the right bird because Raven was sitting in a tree singing his baby's song. Carefully, Father Bunting landed in Raven's tree, waited a moment, then swooped down and snatched his son's song from the thief.

As usual, the baby was crying when Father Bunting arrived back at the nest. He was pretty proud, and Mother Bunting was overjoyed. She sang the baby his song and he fell asleep.

Even today, when snow buntings see a raven, they stop singing for fear the raven might steal their song away. [Russia]

---

* snow bunting: a finch of northern regions. In Winter, seen in the United States and Europe, especially during snowstorms. Mainly white in color.

❧ Home Sweet Home ☙

There once was a farmer who lived in a tiny house with his wife and six children. Everyone usually talked at once. Sometimes the house was so noisy that the farmer would sit holding his hands over his ears. He was miserable, so miserable that one day he visited his rabbi for comfort. He asked, "Rabbi, please, could you help me? I can't stand the noise in my house. No one ever stops talking. No matter what I do, they keep talking."

The rabbi thought a moment. "Do you raise chickens?" he asked.

The farmer scowled, "Well, yes, but what does that have to do with it?"

"I want you to go home and move your chickens into the house to live with you," the rabbi said very seriously.

The farmer could hardly believe his ears, but he did what the rabbi instructed because, after all, the rabbi was a wise man. When he let his three chickens in the house, it was absolute bedlam. The children loved it. They tried to play catch the chicken, but the chickens didn't want to be caught. Chicken feathers flew everywhere as the birds scurried under beds and tables. After several days of even more noise and messy chickens, the farmer decided to return to the rabbi.

"Rabbi, please," the farmer begged. "I can't stand all this noise and confusion."

The rabbi looked kindly at him and said, "Do you have a goat?"

"Yes, I have a goat," the farmer answered. The rabbi paid no attention to the quiver in the farmer's voice and told him to take the goat inside the house to live.

Bewildered but obedient, the farmer went home, untied his goat, and took the animal into the house. The noise of his wife, the kids, and the chickens scared the goat so much that it knocked over tables, chairs and anything else that was in its way. The farmer's wife was furious, but the children thought it was great fun.

The next day the farmer decided he couldn't stand to live this way and again visited the rabbi. "I can't stand that house!" he yelled. "It's still noisy! We have chicken feathers in our food, and now the house smells. Would you *please* help me?"

Once more the rabbi did not comfort the farmer. He only told him to go home and take his cow into the house. But when the farmer did, his wife wouldn't cook and sat outside the house all night.

The farmer prepared dinner. By the time he fed the children, the cow, the goat, and the chickens, he had decided to return to the rabbi a fourth time.

Before the farmer could say anything, the rabbi said, "I think it is time for you to remove the animals from your house." The farmer ran home and told his wife. They moved the animals outside and enjoyed the evening together. It wasn't exactly quiet. After all, six children and two adults in a one room house is bound to be noisy, but with the animals gone, it was "Home Sweet Home!" to the farmer and his family. [Jewish Folklore]

Family Affair

In the 1860's, philanthropist* Horace Norton, founder of Norton College, was given a cigar by Ulysses Simpson Grant, the 18th president of the United States. It is said that Norton decided not to smoke the cigar but to keep it as a memento of the meeting. On his death the cigar passed to his son and then, in turn, to his son's son, Winstead.

In 1932 Winstead attended a Norton College reunion in Chicago. As he delivered a speech to the audience, he lit Grant's cigar, remarking: "As I light this cigar with trembling hand, it is not alone a tribute to him whom you call founder, but also to that titan** among statesmen who was never too exalted to be a friend, who was..." Bang! The cigar exploded. It had taken some 70 years, but Grant had finally played his joke.

---

* philanthropist: one who gives gifts of money to promote human welfare

** titan: one who stands out for greatness in human achievement

The Hare and the Tortoise

The old tale of the slow and steady tortoise and the swift and clever hare is still enjoyed by listeners and readers everywhere. However, most who enjoy the tale picture not the hare and the tortoise in their minds, but a little turtle and a cute rabbit.

A hare is no "dumb bunny." It has many enemies that it can outrun, such as coyotes, bobcats, foxes, and dogs, at up to 40 miles per hour. Its long back legs allow it to leap 18 to 22 feet, and its 7-inch ears can be controlled separately, which allows it to pinpoint a sound of danger.

The tortoise is the same slow, plodding character of folklore but with a few exceptions. It is able to dig a burrow to hide from the Summer sun and the cold of Winter. Sometimes these burrows are large enough to shelter 20 tortoises. It has a patterned shell, like a turtle, that's at least a foot long, and it has scaly, thick front and back legs. It weighs at least 20 pounds.

But, of course, no one would create a story about a tired looking, antique tortoise and a rabbit with ears too long for its body that leaps like a kangaroo.

❧ The Man with a Fake Nose ❧

Long ago (during the sixteenth century, to be exact), a young man, an expert at math, got into a hot and heavy argument with another young man about who was the best mathematician. They were both so determined to win that they pulled out their swords. Tycho Brahe, a Dane, was the real loser, because a good part of his nose was sliced off.

But Tycho wasted very little time on self-pity. He had a new nose made from gold, silver, copper, and wax. To finish it, he had the nose painted the color of flesh, and glued in the proper place, and wore it until his death at 54 years of age.

Tycho Brahe was a young man of courage even before he lost his nose. One day he observed a partial eclipse of the sun. It was so exciting to him that he decided to become an astronomer. When his parents heard of this, they were furious. They wanted him to become a lawyer. This argument continued for a long time, until finally, against his parents' wishes, Tycho spent his life gazing at the stars.

In 1572 he observed an exploding star, the brightest to have been seen in 1,000 years. His discovery of this exciting, important event dismissed forever the Greek idea that the heavens were unchanging. Eventually, the exploded star was named Tycho's star.

❧ The Wolf, the Fox, and the Otter ❧

Wolf, Fox, and Otter were feeding a pig potatoes, turnips, and apples. They were trying to fatten the pig so that one day they could have roast pork for dinner.

One day, Wolf said, "I can hardly wait to eat my pig."

Fox said, "What do you mean, your pig? It's our pig."

Otter just smiled. "Time will tell whose pig it is."

The moment the pig died, Wolf was ready to gobble it up, and Fox was, too. But Otter said, "No!" Don't eat that pig yet. He needs to be washed. We'll get sick if we eat dirty food."

Wolf and Fox agreed, so the three of them dragged the pig to a pond to wash it. Wolf held the back legs and Fox held the tail. Otter, who was a champion swimmer, dove into the water, grabbed the pig's neck, and pulled for all he was worth. He pulled so hard that Wolf and Fox began slipping in the mud and finally fell into the pond. When Wolf and Fox let go of the pig, Otter went swimming away to an island in the middle of the pond.

Wolf and Fox spent the rest of the day watching Otter with greedy eyes as he feasted on the whole pig all by himself. [France]

❦ Rabbit and His Friends ❧

There once was a rabbit who was very popular. He had many friends. When he heard the hounds approaching one day, he ran to his friends for help. "Bull, Bull, get rid of the hounds with your horns," the rabbit pleaded.

The bull replied, "I am very sorry, but I have a date."

The goat made excuses and sent the rabbit to the ram.

The ram replied, "Of course, I can't help you. Hounds have been known to eat sheep, you know."

The rabbit then beseeched the calf as a last hope, who regretted that he was unable to help because so many older animals more knowing than he had declined the task.

By this time the hounds were quite near, so the rabbit took to his heels and, luckily, escaped. And he learned that he who has many friends, sometimes has no friends. [United States]

Spring Rains

Johnny Whitecoat was a cowboy who drove cattle on the Chisholm Trail. One day while in the small town of Bixby in Indian Territory, Johnny realized he had lost some of his steers. So he climbed on his horse and went looking for them. During his search he happened onto Sandra Dee's land.

Sandra Dee was sitting at the kitchen table drinking a cup of coffee when she saw a strange man in her field. Sandra Dee arose from the table, grabbed her gun, and just as bold as brass, went out the door, pointed the gun at Johnny, and said, "Stick 'em up or I'll plug ya'." All Johnny did was laugh. He laughed so hard and so long that finally, Sandra Dee laughed, too. That was the beginning of a wonderful friendship and each time Johnny went to Indian Territory, he stopped to see Sandra Dee. And one time when he stopped, they got married.

The following year they had a baby boy. Johnny was so proud of his son that he told anyone who would listen, "I'm only makin' one more trip on the trail and then I'm stayin' home with my wife and kid." Johnny left for his last trip just before the Spring rains. One night, after a week of bad Spring storms, Sandra Dee was upstairs getting the baby ready for bed when she heard the porch floor creak. Then she heard the front door squeak and a voice call, "Sandra Dee, I'm comin' to get you."

Frightened, Sandra Dee bolted the bedroom door, took a sheet off the bed and made a sling from it. She put the boy in the sling and lowered him out the window to the ground. Then she jumped out herself, picked up the baby and ran to her horse and carriage.

When she reached the road, she whipped her horse to make it run faster and faster. Sandra Dee raced to get across the Snake River to a friend's house. The river, about to overflow, roared so loudly it scared Sandra Dee's horse and made it difficult to keep the animal on the road. Suddenly, she heard hoofbeats behind her. She was certain it was her intruder and whipped her horse to run faster. She stayed ahead, but as she approached the edge of the bridge her horse stopped. He wouldn't move. Sandra Dee jumped from the carriage, grabbed the reins and began walking the horse across the bridge. When they reached the middle, the river washed out the bridge and all were lost.

Even today, the old timers in Bixby will tell you that if you cross the Snake River after midnight, you will see the ghost of Sandra Dee sitting on the west bank waiting for Johnny. And if you listen carefully, you can hear a baby crying. And that is how the bridge became known as "The Crying Baby Bridge." [Pat Nelson]

⚜ Bear and Vixen ⚜

Vixen* loved to play tricks on Bear. It was easy to trick Bear because he wasn't as smart as he looked. One day, Vixen went down to the lake and there was Bear. He was splashing the water with his paw. Vixen had an idea that Bear was trying to catch a fish, but he didn't let on. He only asked, "What are you doing here, Bear? Swimming?"

Bear answered, "Oh, no, Vixen. I was trying to catch a carp."**

"I think you need a little help, Bear."

"Well, I guess I do, but I don't know what I need."

Vixen stood there a moment pretending to think, and then said suddenly, "I have it. You drink all the water out of the lake and then we'll share the fish."

"That's a great idea, Vixen. Why didn't I think of that?" Without another word Bear began drinking.

When Vixen saw how fast Bear could drink, he said to himself, Bear isn't much on thinking, but he's sure big on drinking.

When the lake was nearly drained, Vixen stayed close to Bear. As soon as he saw the carp, Vixen grabbed it and ran. Bear was angry and wanted to run after Vixen and get the carp from him, but he just couldn't run because he was so full of water. [Russia]

---

* vixen: a female fox
** carp: a soft-finned freshwater fish

⚜ Pandora's Box ⚜

Long ago, when the world was young, there was no such thing as trouble. One day, Epimetheus brought home a strange and beautiful box. He told his wife, Pandora, "Mercury, the messenger of the gods, sent it, and it must not be opened. Pandora, you must remember this. If you forget and it is opened, we will have trouble."

Pandora understood what her husband told her, but she was a very curious woman. One day, her curiosity got the best of her. She could not resist the temptation to see what was inside the box. She untied the golden knot, and instantly the room was filled with hundreds of horrible, insect-like creatures. Quickly Pandora put the lid back, but not before all the troubles on Earth had been set free: sickness, jealousy, hatred, and lies to fill the world. She held the lid down with her hand, but then she heard the cry, "Help!" from the box. When she pulled up one corner to peek inside, she found a tiny creature with golden wings who said, "My name is Hope."

Quickly, Pandora covered the box with the lid, trapping Hope inside. And Hope has been there ever since, comforting humans in spite of all their troubles. [Greece]

❧ Hunting the Owl ❧

Walter was only seven years old and had lived on a farm just a few weeks. One afternoon, as he walked through the woods near his house, he came upon an owl that was sound asleep. At first he was scared. He had never seen an owl before. But as he watched, he wondered why the owl was sleeping during the day. Then he remembered what his father had told him—that owls sleep during the day so they can hunt at night.

Walter's parents had told him he could have a pet, and Walter wondered whether an owl would be a good pet. The more he thought about it, the more he realized he better try to catch the owl before it awakened. Walter moved very carefully toward the owl. He moved closer and closer, until he was standing under the limb of the tree where the owl sat. Slowly, carefully, he reached up to the owl and grabbed it by the legs. The legs felt strange in his hands, but he got a good grip on them.

Suddenly, the owl awoke and began fighting Walter. Its eyes were wild and its cry was horrifying. The bird used all its strength to struggle against him. Walter, numb with fear, just hung on.

Walter never knew what happened next. He only knew that fear overwhelmed him. Maybe the owl gouged him—he doesn't remember. He only knows he became terrified. But in spite of his fear, he wouldn't let go of the bird. He hurled it to the ground and stomped on it until it was dead.

Walter was so shocked and ashamed by his own behavior that he was a grown man before he ever told anyone about it. After that, for many years, every time he told the tale he cried. He felt such regret that he never killed another living creature in his life.

However, he didn't forget about animals. He spent his life drawing pictures of them. I know you know who he was. His name was Walt Disney.

MAY

May

May's not brilliant.
She can't speak Latin
But she can drape poles
In ribboned satin.
Leave baskets of flowers
At her neighbor's door,
Serve strawberry shortcake,
And what is more
She can sing and dance,
Attend mayfests, and then
Praise the armed services,
Both women and men.
Sometimes she'll stir up
A storm that you'll hate.
But always remember,
May loves to celebrate.

—Pat Nelson

❧ The Goddess of the Corn ❧

Long, long ago, the goddess of the corn lived by the Little Missouri River in North Dakota. She was called the Old Woman Who Never Dies. One day she moved south, where she owned much land. She knew the mice and the moles would help her work her land. Two deer and a large flock of blackbirds kept watch over her fields.

The water birds were her messengers. When she sent them north, the Mandan Indians knew Spring had come. When she sent the geese, the Indians planted corn. When she sent the swans, they planted gourds. When she sent the ducks, they planted beans.

Before planting the corn, the Indians danced the Corn Dance in honor of the goddess. Each woman carried a stick that had an ear of corn fastened to the end. They sat in a circle, and each woman planted her ear of corn. Then they danced while the old men played the drums and sang. When the corn was harvested, they had another dance. Each woman carried a corn stalk, just as it had been pulled out of the ground.

When the water birds returned to the south, the Mandan Indians sent a prayer with them to the goddess: "Do not send the Winter too soon, so that the game leaves our country too early and we do not have enough meat." [Native American]

❧ Buster the Dog ❧

Buster was Grandpa's favorite dog. Even though the dog was considered too small to take hunting, Grandpa said Buster was a great rabbit hunter. He was able to quickly get in and out of places where Grandpa's expensive hunting dogs wouldn't dare venture.

The day that Buster ran into an ax that had been left in a stump and sliced the dog in two—right down the middle—Grandpa just happened to walk by. He picked up the two pieces of the dog, wrapped them in a blanket, put them in his truck and raced to Dr. Bates' office. Dr. Bates was a practical man. Rather than sew Buster together, which would take hours and be life threatening, Dr. Bates used his sticking salve to glue Buster together in a matter of minutes.

They always say, "Haste makes waste," and in this case I think it was probably true. Dr. Bates mistakenly glued two legs up and two legs down. But when Buster recovered, it didn't really bother him very much. He still enjoyed chasing rabbits, but now that he was improperly glued together, he just ran on two legs until he was tired and then switched to his other two.

And Grandpa is still prouder of Buster than he is of his expensive hunting dogs. [American Tall Tale]

❧ A Jack Tale ❧

Jack was the young commander of a torpedo boat during World War II. One day in August 1943, his crew was surprised by a Japanese destroyer in the South Pacific. Complete chaos erupted on the boat as dishes, paper, and odds and ends flew through the air, and flames leaped and water spilled onto the deck. The crew members abandoned ship to survive.

In the sea, Jack rallied his men to swim to the nearest island around 3 miles away. When he realized one man was wounded too severely to make it, Jack put the end of the sailor's life jacket between his teeth and towed the man to shore.

Several days passed before they were rescued. During that time they ate whatever they could find growing on the island, which wasn't much. When the search party finally landed, the torpedo boat crew heard a voice in the jungle call, "Hey, Jack, where are ya?"

After a moment of silence, Jack called, "Where have you been?"

Instead of answering the question, the rescuer called back, "We've got some food for you." Jack, who was starving, denied his hunger pangs in spite of the possibility of a meal.

Still playing it cool, he answered, "No, thanks. I just ate a coconut."

John F. Kennedy, called "Jack" or "JFK" by those who knew him well, became our 35th president and the youngest man to ever be elected to the office. He was 43. He is also considered our wittiest president. Lincoln told many jokes that endeared him to the people, but Kennedy's humor was the clever manipulation of conversation. He could quickly make a joke of any situation. Today, when we think of Jack Kennedy, our first thought often is of his terrible death by an assassin's bullet. But our second thought is of a president with a wonderful wit.

⚜ Señor Coyote and the Dogs ⚜

One day when Señor Coyote, the trickster, was walking in the valley, two dogs jumped out from behind a boulder and started to chase him. Coyote ran and ran as fast as he could. It seemed the dogs were beginning to lag behind when suddenly two more dogs joined the chase. The barking attracted more dogs, and soon Coyote was actually running to save his life.

Luck was with him. As he rounded a large boulder, he came upon a cave with an opening just large enough for him to slip through but too small for the dogs. Once inside, he caught his breath and then thought about the race. He felt pretty good about winning that race.

He said, "Feet, what did you do to help me?"

His feet answered, "We jumped the rocks and bushes and got you here."

"Good feet," said Coyote. "And ears, what did you do?"

"We listened to the right and the left."

"Good ears," said Coyote. "And eyes, what did you do?"

"We saw the cave."

"Good eyes," said Coyote. "What a marvelous fellow I am to have such fine feet, eyes, and ears." Coyote felt so good about himself that he patted himself on the back, and that's when he remembered his tail. "Tail, I don't remember you doing anything."

"That's right," said his tail. "I wanted those dogs to catch you. I motioned to them to come and have at you."

Coyote was so angry he bit his tail and yelled, "*Silencio!* I'm going to fix you. You tried to help them catch me, so I'm putting you out the door where they can chew you up." Coyote stuck his tail out the cave hole, and the dogs that were waiting grabbed hold of it and pulled Coyote out. Coyote came to a tragic end. [Mexico]

❧ The Golden Apple ❧

There was once a king who announced he would give away a golden apple to the person who could tell him the biggest lie. All sorts of people tried, but the king always shook his head and said, "That's all very well, but it could be true."

One day, a young man holding a barrel in his hand said to the king, "Oh, mighty monarch, I've come for my gold coins."

"What gold coins?" asked the king.

"The barrel of gold coins you borrowed from me last week!"

"I certainly never borrowed a barrel of gold coins from you. That is a lie!"

"If it's a lie, then give me the golden apple," said the young man.

The king stopped short. "Wait a moment! You're quite right! I've just remembered!"

"That suits me fine, my king. Then give me the barrel of gold coins!"

The king realized he had been outwitted and gave the young man the golden apple. [Persia]

❧ Why We Can't Look at the Sun ❧

In ancient China there was a young man who lived on the sun, and his two sisters lived on the moon. These two beautiful sisters were artists with embroidery needles. They embroidered dragons, flowers, butterflies, and birds in tiny, tiny stitches all over their clothes. Always they could be seen sitting in their palace garden stitching in the light of the moon.

The sisters became famous. Each night the people on Earth would climb the highest mountains in order to see these sisters better. And from their palace the sisters could see what was happening on the Earth. However, they did not like being stared at, especially by men.

"We cannot stay here, my sister," said one of the moon maidens.

And the other answered, "I know, and I have thought of a plan. We will let our brother live here and we will take his place on the sun."

When they asked their brother to move, he laughed. "Silly creatures! During the day, many more people gaze at the sun than stare at the moon at night. You will double your problem instead of solving it."

"No! No! Brother," one of the moon maidens cried. "We have a plan to stop the staring." And then the maidens both began to weep. The brother took pity on them and agreed to move. In less time than it takes to drink a cup of tea, the women were on the sun embroidering their silks and satins.

The Earth people were a little shocked when they couldn't see the sisters on the moon. When word got around that they had moved to the sun, the people went to gaze at them, but they felt a terrible pricking in their eyes. Some said it was only the strong rays of the sun, but others maintained it was the 70 embroidery needles of the moon maidens pricking the eyes of all who stared. And the sisters' plan worked! [China]

⚕ The First Strawberries ⚕

One day the first Cherokee woman and the first Cherokee man got into an argument. The woman became so angry that she left and began walking toward the Sun Land. The man was very upset, and he tried to follow her.

Sun took pity on the man and asked him if he would like to have his wife back. The man answered, "Yes." So Sun used his magic to cause huckleberries to grow along the path where she was walking. But she never noticed them. Sun tried again, with blackberries. She didn't pay any attention to these either.

Sun decided these bushes grew too high. The woman was upset, too, and walked with her head down. So Sun created a low bush with big, ripe, red berries on it. They were so large and so beautiful that the woman couldn't help but notice them. She bent down and picked one and put it in her mouth. It was so delicious she ate another and another. No wonder—these were the first strawberries ever known.

She picked as many as she could carry and brought them back to share with her husband. And they lived together for ever and ever. [Native American]

⚕ El Pajaro-Cu ⚕

When the world was young, all birds had feathers as they do today, except one. El Pajaro-Cu, as the featherless one was called, had to fly about the sky as naked as your hand.

Eagle, chief of the birds, thought this was shameful. At the birds' council meeting, he said, "We must put this bird out of the country."

Dove took pity on El Pajaro-Cu and timidly said, "Why don't we each donate him a feather?"

Crow said, "A fine idea."

But Peacock cried, "No, he will be too beautiful with red, yellow, blue, black, brown, orange, and green feathers and will become too vain."

Owl said, "Nonsense, you're just jealous."

Eagle said, "Well, we can't leave it this way."

Finally, it was agreed that each bird would give him a feather. When El Pajaro-Cu was clothed he went to the pool to see how he looked and screamed, "I am beautiful! I am marvelous! I am wonderful!" Peacock had been right. That bird became so vain it didn't want to be with any of the other birds, and one day it just flew away and never came back.

All the birds went to look for him but could never find him. People say even today when the birds in the forest keep calling and calling, they are still calling for El Pajaro-Cu. [Mexico]

❧ Why a Cat Eats First ☙

Long ago, there was a cat and a mouse who were friends. One day, the mouse watched the cat sneak up on another mouse, grab it, and eat it. "Yuk," said the mouse. "Don't you wash your hands and face before you eat?"

The cat looked a little ashamed and then began to lick her paws and wash her face, as cats do today.

She was so busy with her washing that the mouse got tired of waiting and very quietly slipped away. Finally, when the cat decided she was absolutely clean, she looked up, expecting to have the mouse for company, but he was gone. The cat looked everywhere, but no matter where she looked, she couldn't find the mouse.

It was a good lesson for the cat; since she was nobody's fool, she never forgot it. Even today, a cat always eats first and washes later. [African-American]

❧ Silent Darkness ☙

Seven-year-old Helen threw herself onto the floor. Kicking and screaming, she threw a terrible tantrum. That day she was angry. Some days she was mischievous, like the day she locked her mother in the closet and hid the key. Not until evening, when her father put a ladder up to the closed window, had Helen's mother been released from her tiny prison.

The neighbors often talked about the Kellers' little girl Helen. Some said, "She's just spoiled. Her parents feel sorry for her. That's why she behaves like that."

One woman really believed Helen was mean-spirited. She was visiting the Kellers one day when Helen found her baby sister sleeping in her doll carriage. She was so furious she dumped the carriage over. Out spilled the crying baby sister. Helen's mother rescued the baby, and Helen's father tried to comfort his little girl, who cried louder than the baby.

Helen Keller lived in silent darkness, not only blind but also deaf. She was born normal, but at 19 months she developed a terrible fever. For many days she was near death. Then one day, just as suddenly as it had arrived, the fever disappeared. And with it went Helen's sight and hearing.

But Helen Keller learned to read, and she found a way to hear. She graduated from Radcliffe College and lectured all over the world. She inspired the blind to see and the deaf to hear. She made a movie, and her autobiography was a best-seller.

How was she able to do this? She had a wonderful, dedicated teacher— Anne Sullivan. But that's another story.

❧ A Master Teacher ❧

Anne Sullivan accepted quite a challenge when she agreed to come and live with the Kellers and be Helen's teacher. She began by putting a doll in one of Helen's hands and then writing "d-o-l-l" with her finger on Helen's other palm. Helen learned to retrace "d-o-l-l" with her finger, but she couldn't learn what the word *doll* meant. Helen learned to trace many words, but even Anne wondered if she would ever learn to connect them.

One day, Anne, desperately trying to teach Helen that "m-u-g" and the "m-i-l-k" in the mug had different names, almost dragged Helen outside to the pump, for she had an idea she was excited about. She handed Helen the mug at the pump, pumped cold water into it, and then spelled "w-a-t-e-r" in Helen's hand. Suddenly, Helen understood! She understood that "w-a-t-e-r" was something … "d-o-l-l" was something … "h-a-t" was something! Everything had a name—and every name could be spelled in her hand. The whole idea was so powerful that Helen ran all over the yard touching—touching roses … a watering can … a shovel … pansies. Touching … touching … touching. And with everything she touched, Anne Sullivan was there to spell it for her. At last, exhausted, Helen fell to the ground and pounded it with her hand, and Anne Sullivan fell to the ground, too, and spelled "g-r-o-u-n-d."

That night was the first time Helen ever showed any love for her teacher. She gave Anne a hug and a kiss for helping her to see the world. From that day forward, they were Master Teacher and Master Student.

⚡ Sky Dog ⚡

When the moon passes between the sun and the Earth, we call that an eclipse. It only lasts for a few minutes, but sometimes it can become quite dark and very frightening, especially if you don't know why it's happening. The ancient Chinese knew very little about the solar system. Most of their knowledge came from the old stories that had been handed down. They believed that when the sun was blocked out except for a small, bright rim of light, Sky Dog, who lived on a special star, was trying to swallow the sun.

One day a soothsayer, who is someone who speaks the truth, warned the king that very soon there would be a solar eclipse. The king announced to all the people to beware. When the day came, all the servants in the houses brought out their drums. Some went right into the street with cymbals, rattles, and pans to beat on with sticks.

They stared at the sky. It became darker and darker. When it looked as though the sun was disappearing down the throat of Sky Dog, they pounded as hard as they could on their drums. They banged their pans and crashed their cymbals harder and harder. Some people covered their ears. Children cried, and nurses picked them up and rocked them in their arms.

It grew darker and darker until just a tiny rim of bright light showed. Everyone was so frightened they began screaming. The adults screamed as loud as the children. The servants beat their drums harder and harder, and their cymbals crashed over and over.

Gradually the sky became lighter, and finally, Sky Dog became frightened. He coughed up the sun, and the sun shone brighter than ever in the sky. The children went off to play again. The servants went back to work. And the king and all the other adults went home to rest. [China]

The Angel of the Battlefield

Clara was little and shy. Six older brothers and sisters made her cry. They thought "shy" was pretty strange. Her mother said, "Clara is shy because she is at least 10 years younger than her brothers and sisters." Her father said, "Clara needs a friend." Timid and frail, Clara spent most of her time alone.

Attempting to correct Clara's shyness, her mother gave her much responsibility. At 11, Clara nursed her brother through an illness. When Clara was 15, her mother was so confident of Clara's abilities that she managed to get the girl a job as a schoolteacher. Teaching frightened Clara, but the years of working closely with her mother paid off. Her shyness slipped away as she taught with courage and discipline for 18 years.

When she tired of teaching, Clara became a Civil War nurse. Applying the same courage and discipline, she insisted upon going right to the front lines. It was there that she was nicknamed the "Angel of the Battlefield" because she comforted and saved the lives of so many soldiers.

After the war, Clara learned of the European Red Cross and led a fight for 11 years to establish a branch in the United States. Clara finally became director of the Red Cross in 1881 and held the job for 23 years.

Yes, Clara Barton was a shy child, but as you can see, she never let shyness interfere with what she wanted to do with her life.

The Chef's Revenge

You'd expect that the chef at the Moon Lake Lodge restaurant in Saratoga Springs, New York, would be French as the restaurant was so famous for its delicious French food. However, the chef, George Crum, was not French, nor had he ever been to Paris. Chef George Crum was an Indian chief who took great pride in being able to prepare many French dishes.

One evening a very, very rich and well-known customer, Cornelius Vanderbilt, came into the restaurant and ordered french fries, a dish he had just tasted in Paris, where it was the new rage. When the waiter brought Mr. Vanderbilt his plate of french fries, Vanderbilt took one look and complained loudly, "For heaven's sake, man! I don't want these big thick things. Take them back. I want thin french fries. Your chef should know how to do it."

The fries went back to the kitchen in a hurry. The chef made another batch, much thinner this time. However, once again, Mr. Vanderbilt insisted on a french fry that was more like the ones he had eaten in France. "Thin!" he shouted. "Make them thin!"

Vanderbilt's insistence made the chef so angry that this time he sliced the potatoes so thin you could almost see through them. When fried, they looked like a plate of brown shingles. The chef covered them liberally with salt and brought them to Mr. Vanderbilt himself, hoping to further insult Vanderbilt with this unpalatable looking pile of fried potatoes. Mr. Vanderbilt didn't let the appearance bother him and began eating, then smiled. "They're not as good as Paris, but they're pretty darn good."

What Mr. Vanderbilt liked, Mr. Vanderbilt got. The dish was immediately put on the menu of the restaurant. In 1887, the American version of the french fry was included in the White House cookbook. In the 1920s, when peeling and slicing machines were invented, this concoction of an angry Indian chief was available internationally ... and it is still popular today ... the potato chip.

❦ Putting His Best Foot Forward ❧

Jan was born in Dutch Guiana to a native black mother and a wealthy Dutch engineer father. At 19, he decided he wanted to see the world. When the merchant ship he worked on docked in Philadelphia, Jan Ernst Matzeliger decided to give life in the United States a try.

He ended up in Lynn, Massachusetts, working in a shoe factory. In 1877, making a shoe meant the bottom of the shoe had to be sewn to the top by hand, which was a time-consuming, laborious job. Subsequently, Jan invented a machine to do the stitching. After several improvements and some financial backing, he received a patent on his "lasting machine." His machine could sew 150 to 700 pairs of shoes per day, instead of the 50 pairs that could be done by hand. Because of his invention, the U.S. shoe industry was able to step out in front.

Several years later, Jan became ill with tuberculosis and died at the young age of 37. He left his stock in The Lasting Machine Company to the North Congregational Church, the only church in Lynn, Massachusetts, that had not rejected him because of his skin color.

❦ Teenage Literature ❧

Susie loved to write. She loved to write so much that when she was in trouble with her parents they didn't ground her—they took away her typewriter. That was a serious punishment for Susie, who had written two books before she entered high school.

While a student at Will Rogers High School in Tulsa, Oklahoma, she started another book. She didn't like the fiction that was available for teenagers. She wanted to write a story that was realistic for the times. It's rumored that when she was working on it, she came down to breakfast one morning and asked her dad, "If I publish this book, will you buy me a car?"

Everyone at the table snickered, and her dad, sounding very serious, said, "Why, of course, Susie." Little did he know that Susie's book would be published before she graduated.

S. E. Hinton's first published book is still one of the best-selling "youth" or "young adult" novels in history. It is recommended and often required reading in high schools throughout the country. She created a new way to touch the teenage mind. The market was ready for it and the time was right.

S. E. Hinton has received many honors and awards for her writing, but what pleases her most about *The Outsiders* is that it has encouraged a lot of kids to read. They read her other books, too: *That Was Then, This Is Now*; *Rumble Fish*; *Tex*; and *Taming the Star Runner*. She has been a star in the minds of teenage readers and probably will be for a long time to come.

◈ The Pink Ribbon ◈

Once there was a boy named John and a girl named Jane. They lived next door to each other and fell in love when they were children. In first grade, John carried Jane's books to school. Every day Jane wore a pink ribbon tied around her neck. One day John said, "Why in the world do you wear that pink ribbon tied around your neck?"

Jane said, "I'm not telling. Maybe I'll tell you some day, but not today."

Year after year, John and Jane remained close friends, but she would never tell him why she wore that pink ribbon around her neck.

When they graduated from high school, they became engaged. At that time, Jane promised that on their wedding day she would tell John why she wore the pink ribbon around her neck. The wedding day came and went, and John never heard why she wore the pink ribbon around her neck.

Many years passed, but still Jane didn't tell. One day she took to her death bed. John got onto his knees and begged, "Why don't you untie that pink ribbon that is around your neck?"

Finally, Jane said, "All right, I'll tell you. You will have to find out for yourself. You may untie it now."

John did and Jane's head fell off. [United States]

SUMMER

Summer

Sun's on a roll!
She's on top of the world,
Prancing across the sky
In shimmering gold.
She melts clouds in her way,
Gives wind a swift kick,
Acts like she owns the place.

Desperate clouds and wind
Plan equinox party.

—Pat Nelson

❦ The Ant and the Grasshopper ❧

In a field one Summer's day a grasshopper was hopping about, chirping and singing to its heart's content. An ant came by, struggling with an ear of corn. It was much too large for the ant to move, but he kept tugging and pulling at it. The grasshopper was delighted to see the ant because he was lonely. He called, "Ant, Ant, come and sing and talk with me. You always are working, working, working. You work much too hard. Life is fun! Come on and have a good time."

"I can't," said the ant. "I have to store this corn so I'll have something to eat in the Winter."

"Oh, don't be such a spoil sport," the grasshopper taunted. "Just make sure your belly is full now. Winter will take care of itself." But the ant insisted that he had to get his Winter food taken care of.

When the snow came and the Winter winds blew, the grasshopper couldn't find anything to eat. Weak from hunger, he lay on the ground and watched the ant distribute corn to all the other ants. Finally, the grasshopper caught on to the fact that it is best to be prepared for bad days ahead. [Aesop]

❧ The Summer Solstice ❧

When the lingering sun colors the twilight a dusky gold, barrels of dry leaves are ignited and rolled down the mountains to announce the longest day of the year, Midsummer Day, the time of the Summer solstice. Many centuries ago it was the biggest festival on the European continent. Young people loved Midsummer Day because they were allowed to stay up all night on Midsummer Eve to watch the fire barrels bounce down the mountains, then sing and dance around huge bonfires. Some even risked leaping over the fire because they were told it would bring them good luck.

Rome celebrated this festival with races between young people paddling flower-decked boats. There were other races, too, but if the youth didn't like racing, they searched for birds bathing together in streams, and if they were successful, the young people believed they were blessed.

Some Europeans believed fairies could speak with human tongues on this magical night. And if you wanted to see the fairies, you had to rub fern seed on your eyes. It made you invisible. The fairies danced in a ring of 12 flowers, and one of those flowers was the Flower of Happiness. If at midnight you were lucky enough to pick that flower, you could look forward to being happy ever after.

In the Scandinavian countries maypoles were decorated with birth leaves, flowers, strips of colored paper, and eggshells, gilded and strung on a string. In Germany everyone who celebrated went to the woods and gathered boughs and blossoms which they made into wreaths for their heads. In their excitement to celebrate the beginning of Summer, large groups would walk miles through village after village inviting others to join them.

In Finland they still roll their flaming barrels down the mountains to celebrate the Summer solstice, but most of the European Midsummer Day customs have been forgotten.

An Act of Greatness

An old man was dying when he called for his three sons and showed them a jewel. I cannot give it to all of you, so I will give it to the one who can tell me of the finest act of greatness he has ever performed.

The first son said, "Once a man left much money with me. I kept it for him for a long time. When he returned, I gave it all back and did not charge him anything for my service. Wasn't that an act of greatness?"

The old man said, "No, that was honesty, not greatness."

The second son spoke, "Once I was passing a pond and saw a child drowning. With no thought for myself, I jumped in and carried him to his mother. Wasn't this an act of greatness?"

The old man said, "No, that was an act of sympathy, not greatness. To be great, your act must be remarkably uncommon.

Finally, the youngest son spoke. "I was walking near a gorge one night. I saw my enemy lying on the clifftop at the edge of the gorge. He was sound asleep. I could see that if he moved in his sleep, he would fall into the gorge and be killed. I moved towards him quietly, and taking him by both hands, I pulled him to a safe place. Isn't that an act of greatness?"

The old man was very pleased. "Yes," he said, kissing the cheeks of his youngest son. "There is no better act of greatness than doing good to an enemy." And he gave the jewel to the youngest son. [Mexico]

The Lark and Her Young Ones

When the wheat was short and green, a lark made her nest in a field. Her babies grew just as the wheat. Then, one day, a farmer and his son came into the field. The father said, "This wheat is ready for reaping. Contact our neighbors today, so they can help us harvest it."

When the babies heard this, they were frightened. When the mother came home with food for them, they told her what they had heard.

The mother lark was calm. "Don't worry. If he's going to depend on his neighbors for help, this wheat is not going to be reaped very quickly."

A few days later, the farmer and his son were back. The farmer examined the wheat and announced, "If this wheat isn't harvested at once, we shall lose half the crop. Never mind our friends. Tomorrow we will do it ourselves."

When the larks told their mother what they had heard that day, she said, "Then we must move at once. When a man decides to do his own work and not depend on someone else, you can be sure that he will not delay."

When the father and son cut down the wheat the next day, they found an empty nest.

The point: If you want a job well done, do it yourself. [Aesop]

❧ Leopard, Goat, and Yam ❧

A young African decided to move from his village and live on the other side of the river. He had few possessions: a leopard, a goat, and a yam. But he had to think for a long time before he could decide how to get all his possessions across the river safely. Hungry animals crowded into a canoe wouldn't be friendly. If he left the yam with the goat or the leopard with the goat, the goat would eat the yam or the leopard would eat the goat.

After much thought he found a way to solve his problem. He took the goat over first, and then the yam. Then he left the yam and brought the goat back across the river. Then he left the goat while he brought the leopard across. Finally, he went back for the goat. [West Africa]

❧ Fluttering Foreheads ❧

People who work with elephants know that they can trumpet, growl, and even rumble, and now we are told that elephants also make low-frequency sounds. The reason we didn't know about this is because humans cannot hear low-frequency communication.

In 1985 Kathryn Payne, a researcher at Cornell University in New York State, was watching some elephants at the zoo when she noticed that some of the elephants' foreheads fluttered at the same time that she felt a strange throbbing in the air, like a small shock wave. She became suspicious that it was some kind of communication that was not audible to human beings but would be recordable.

After much study, the necessity for elephants to communicate in low-frequency sound was understood. Normal elephant noises do not carry well in the wild, but low-frequency sounds carry great distances. This ability, along with the fact that elephants are known to have a keen sense of hearing (they can recognize the slightest difference in musical notes and have been known to learn as many as 27 verbal commands), explains some questions scientists have asked for years. Until now, people had wondered how the elephant was able to gather many small groups of elephants for a herd. They also wondered how males and females found each other at the right time for breeding. Now they know. It's those fluttering foreheads talking to other fluttering foreheads.

❈ The Mule and the Popcorn ❈

A very successful farmer in Iowa specializes in growing popcorn. A very hot Summer a few years ago, he witnessed a bumper crop in spite of the drought. Naturally, while storing the popcorn, many grains were scattered around the barnyard.

A few days later the thermometer soared. It became so hot that popcorn popped right on the ground. The farmer's pet mule, seeing the barnyard covered with white, imagined it was snow and froze to death. Poor mule!

That same Summer, a neighboring farmer had his popcorn pop right in the fields because the sun was so hot. Kids walking by on their way home from school thought it was snow and tried to make snowballs! Honest!

[American Tall Tale]

If You Care, Honk Your Horn

Childs Park in Northampton, Massachusetts, was established in 1928 and is a beautiful 45-acre woodland with wildflowers and ponds. Today, it is a haven for bird watchers, picnickers and small animals. People in Northampton point to the park with pride because they value its trees for filtering pollution and helping to maintain the ozone layer.

When the city administration announced it was cutting a third of an acre off a corner of Childs Park to be used as a parking lot for school buses and as an aid to traffic safety, three environmentally aware 10-year-old girls made known their opinions about it.

Before their parents knew what was happening, Laura Shepard-Brick, Sarah Crowther, and Ariana Wohl had written a letter to the mayor protesting the change in the park because it meant the removal of 12 to 14 full grown trees. Next, they formed the Children's Committee To Save Our Park. New members helped with painting attention-getting picketing signs like "Beauty Not Speed" and "The Park Is Cool, Dude." When one father suggested they wait until Fall to protest, he found out very quickly that this was their show.

And their show was a smash! They stood on the corner in the heat with signs that asked people to save the trees, consider the environment, and honk their horns if they cared. The newspaper printed their story and members of the committee distributed their signs in downtown store windows. On the third morning of picketing, they were visited by the mayor who came to share with them his solution to the problem before he made it public. His solution was simple. The mayor had found a different location for the school bus parking lot, had asked the traffic department to prohibit left hand turns at the corner in question, and had formed a safety task force to inspect other dangerous intersections. When the mayor finished talking everyone cheered, including the mayor.

Now that it's over, the Children's Committee To Save Our Park feels proud and accomplished. They still argue about the number of honks they received—the figure is someplace around 500—but in quieter moments they wonder why the city responded so quickly. Laura has concluded that "maybe they listened to us more just because we're kids."

❦ The Three Fishes ❧

After looking over a pond one day, some fishermen decided there was plenty of fish in it, and they made plans to fish together the next day.

Three fish had heard the fishermen talking. "Don't put off 'til tomorrow what you can do today," the first fish said to himself and he swam out of the pond through a small hole in the dike.

The second fish did not worry much about the fishermen. "One is always wiser in the morning," he said to himself. But in the morning, he was a bit shocked to find that the fishermen had blocked all the holes in the dike. With a little creative thinking, the fish found a solution. He swam to the surface of the pond, turned upside down, and then floated, pretending to be dead.

The fishermen shook their heads when they saw what looked like a dead fish, and they threw the fish on the dike for the birds. The first moment they weren't looking, the fish flapped himself over to the edge of the dike and then into the stream and freedom.

The third fish had taken no notice of the fishermen's words. "Things will work out somehow," he said to himself. "They always do." And he was still saying that when he was caught in the fishermen's net. [Syria]

❦ The Dog That Talked ❧

A man was entering a hotel one day. As he stepped onto the porch, he saw a sheepdog lying beside the door. Suddenly, the sheepdog looked up and said, "Good morning!" The man thought he was hearing things, but when he walked closer to the dog, the old sheepdog again said, "Good morning."

When the man was inside, he said to the hotel clerk, "Did you know that big sheepdog outside just said good morning to me?"

The hotel clerk laughed, "Oh, no, sir, you must be mistaken."

"I'll have you know I am not mistaken," said the man. "My hearing is quite good."

The hotel clerk stopped a minute and was thoughtful. Then he smiled and said, "I know what happened. That old sheepdog doesn't talk, but the little white terrier that sleeps in the rocking chair is a ventriloquist." [Great Britain]

❧ What a Wonderful Bird the Mosquito Is ❧

As a hunter tracked a deer deep in the northern Minnesota woods, he came upon a swarm of mosquitoes. Within seconds they were flying inside his ears and up his nose. The poor man swatted them as fast as he could and started running.

When he came to a clearing, he took refuge under a huge iron kettle, the kind the army once used. For a few minutes he felt safe, but the mosquitoes were so determined to get him that they drove their stingers right through the iron. The hunter, thinking quickly, pulled a hammer from his bag and riveted the stingers as they came through the kettle.

That poor hunter thought he was pretty smart, and he was, but the mosquitoes were smarter. Since they were attached so securely to the kettle, they took off into the air like birds taking the kettle with them.

There were a number of sitings that day, up and down the Mississippi River, of a flying kettle. Everyone knew it was a joke, because kettles can't fly. However, a few days later, a strange phenomena was reported in South America. It seems a kettle was seen falling through the sky, nearly hitting a plane, and finally falling into the ocean. [American Tall Tale]

❧ A Writing Teacher ❧

Barthe's first strong memory of writing was the day she finished her first story and followed her mother around the house reading the story to her. At 14 she began to write poems about her family and friends. She worried her brothers with her poems. They were afraid she might tell something about them that shouldn't be told. When she announced she was writing an autobiography, they each had a private talk with her. She finally gave up the idea.

Barthe loved writing. She loved books, and she loved people. It seemed to her that teaching was the place for her to be. On her first job, her brain worked overtime finding ways to interest her junior high students. She wrote a paragraph a week on the blackboard about some student in class, and that was the spelling lesson. Later, she continued writing on the blackboard. Paragraph by paragraph, a piece of fiction emerged. One student got so involved in the story, she wondered when Elsie (the story character) was going to join their class. These days, Barthe doesn't teach school but acts as a therapist for kids who need help.

Teaching and counseling are probably the reasons that Barthe DeClements was able to write *Nothing Fair in Fifth Grade* and *How Do You Lose Those Ninth Grade Blues?* in such a realistic way.

❦ The Innkeeper's Mistake ❦

In the years around 1800, there wasn't a railroad in the world. In the United States people didn't even travel by road much because the roads were so crooked and muddy and rough. Anybody who had to go from one city to another usually went on horseback with his or her clothing carried in saddlebags.

One day some men were sitting by the door of an inn in Baltimore when they saw a horseman coming down the road. As the rider got closer, they recognized him as old Farmer Mossback, in from the backwoods and spattered with mud. The rider tied his horse in front of the inn and went inside to the desk. "Have you a room for me here?" he asked. The desk clerk was also the owner and prided himself on keeping a first-class inn. He feared his guests would not like the rough-looking traveller who was dressed like someone from the country. So he answered, "No, sir. Everything is full. Only place I could put you would be the barn." The traveller nodded and left for Planter's Tavern to see about a room there.

About an hour later, a well-dressed gentleman came into the inn. "I wish to see Tom Jefferson, the vice-president of the United States."

The innkeeper said, "Come on. Don't try to kid me."

The gentleman was patient. "I am not trying to be funny. Mr. Jefferson told me he intended to stay at this inn. He should have arrived about an hour ago."

"I'm sorry," answered the innkeeper. "The only man who tried to book a room this morning was an old fellow from the backwoods."

"Did he have reddish hair? And was he tall?" questioned the gentleman.

"Well, he was terribly covered with mud, but I guess I'd say he did have reddish hair, and he was tall. I sent him to Planter's Inn. Do you suppose that really was the vice-president?"

When the gentleman answered, "Yes," the innkeeper shouted orders to the help about fixing the best room and then he ran to Planter's Tavern and found Mr. Jefferson in the lobby. "Sir, I've come to ask your pardon. You were so covered with mud this morning I thought you were some old farmer. Please come back. The best room will be waiting for you."

"No," answered Mr. Jefferson. "A farmer is as good as any other man, and where there's no room for a farmer, there can be no room for me."

⚘ The Stolen Corn ⚘

There once was a steward* who took home a pocketful of corn each evening which he had stolen from his master's barn during the day. By this means, he had gathered enough grain to sow an acre of ground.

When the corn was full and ripe, the steward made arrangements for reapers to harvest his corn. The night before his acre was to be reaped, he viewed it in the light of a full moon. Suddenly, the moon became dark. A flock of crows blocked its light as they descended on the cornfield in great numbers. The steward shouted and screamed, but could not scare them away before each grabbed a stalk of corn.

The steward was angry and disheartened, but, he thought, they didn't get it all. There will be enough for me since, by tomorrow night, all the grain will be reaped.

But the steward was wrong. When the reapers came to the field the next morning, not a stalk remained. The crows had carried every stalk across the river during the night and put each in the master's barn.

It is said that while the crows worked, they were heard chanting:

"Hurry along, hurry along, hurry along, go faster

Never rob, never rob, never rob, your master."

And whenever the steward went to the field on a night when the moon was full, he could hear those crows. [Germany]

---

* steward: an employee of a large farm who supervises employees, rents, and keeps accounts

❧ Sometimes Success Is Hard to Catch ❧

It seemed to everybody, including Harland, that he did everything wrong. First, he quit school when he was only 14. The best job he could find was as a farmhand, but it didn't last long. He hated it. So Harland lied about his age to join the army, but he hated that too. As soon as his commitment was fulfilled, he quit.

He heard the railroads were hiring and knocked on Southern Railroad's door to apply for a job. The company hired him to be a railroad locomotive fireman. It was the first job he had ever liked.

At 18, he got married and was beginning to feel like he was finding himself. However, at about the time he heard he was going to be a father, he was fired from his job. Then his wife decided that the best thing for them was for her to live with her parents. She did, and took all of their belongings with her.

Harland struggled through the Great Depression by getting jobs anywhere he could. He sold insurance and tires. Once, when he had a steady job for awhile, he took a correspondence course in law. But before it was completed, he dropped it. He tried running a filling station and a ferry boat. Both failed, as he knew they would before he had started. When he became quite a bit older, he did find a job in a one-man restaurant. He did it all, and he did it well, but it failed too. Maybe because a new highway was built that bypassed it.

Harland was now old. He looked old, and one of his old customers gave him a birthday cake with 65 candles on it. After a small celebration, Harland thought about his life. It seemed that success had always been out of his reach. Suddenly, he felt old and sad.

The next morning the mailman delivered Harland's first Social Security check for $105. It made him mad. Harland may not have been a success, but he certainly didn't want the government feeling sorry for him. He became so angry that he started his own business with the $105. He developed a secret herb and spice batter to dip his chicken in before he fried it. It was an instant success. The chicken smelled so good while frying that customers who disliked chicken ordered it. Harland's chicken became so popular that he sold franchises* to other people so they could open restaurants like his.

When he was certain he was on the road to real success, he grew a goatee and mustache, he stopped wearing jeans, and he bought himself the most beautiful white suit he could find. His new costume was his way of advertising a very successful business.

Surely you remember pictures of Colonel Harland Sanders on the "Kentucky Fried Chicken" sign. The colonel lived to be 90 years old and enjoyed every minute of those last 25 years.

---

* franchise: the right to market a company's goods or services

❧ The Mouse and the Elephant ❧

A young mouse had just arrived from Athens, where he had acquired a smattering of learning. He was very proud of the little wisdom that he had learned from the books he studied. Puffed up with pride and conceit and anxious to display his wit, one day he addressed an elephant: "Just because you are so large doesn't mean you have to be so pompous in the way you walk. It is true that you are big in size, but this has no value. Really, I think it is a great disadvantage. You can't move nimbly. Your feet are slow and sluggish. But look at me. I am made to fly. I can skip about from place to place. But you have to stop and breathe at each creeping step. Every time I look at you I pity..."

The proud mouse could not finish his speech. Just as he was about to end it, a cat who had grown tired of listening to his words of wisdom pounced upon him and ate him.

The point: Being too critical will get you in trouble every time.
     [Lorenz Pignotti]

❧ Learning the Hard Way ❧

One day Mullah* Nasr-ed-Din was teaching 10 boys. All sat on a hard, clay floor. Their lesson for the day was to read 10 selections from the Koran.** They let their voices chant the words as loudly as possible, in hopes of convincing the Mullah they were studying hard.

Suddenly, two cows passed in the street. The clang of the bells hanging around their necks startled the Mullah. "Boys!" he boomed. The boys' books fell as they came to attention.

"I have a question to ask you," the Mullah began. "Suppose two cows are walking along the street in single file. The last cow tries to move in front of the first cow. The first cow blocks her way. There is a swishing of tails, a tossing of horns, and moos of anger. The second cow pierces the back of the first cow with her sharp horns." The Mullah paused, "Are you all with me?"

The boys chorused, "We are!"

"Then tell me which cow can say, 'I have tail and horns at the same end of my body?'"

One guessed the first cow. Another guessed the second cow. Others guessed both cows. The answer from the Mullah was always, "No!" The boys looked helplessly at one another. No one looked as though they had an inkling of an answer. Finally, they said, "We give up."

The Mullah smiled. It was the moment that made his day. "You boys have forgotten that cows cannot talk."

Once again the boys were aware that Mullah Nasr-ed-Din was more interested in critical thinking than in teaching the Koran. [Iran]

---

*   Mullah: a teacher or judge

** Koran: a book of writings, accepted by Muslims as the divinely inspired, authorized basis for the religious, social, civil, commercial, military, and legal regulations of the Islamic world

❧ A Pioneer Tale ❧

A boy was sent by his parents to the home of some new and well-to-do neighbors. He had been used to deerskins and bull hides for carpets, and when he was invited into the elegantly furnished parlor of his hosts, he was very intimidated. By sidling around the edge of the floor, he managed to get to a chair without walking on a rug that covered most of the floor space. When he left a few moments later, he got out of the room by the same route.

"Well, son, how did you like our new neighbors?" his mother inquired when he returned home.

"Oh," the boy replied, "the lady seemed to be mighty nice, but she is terrible careless-like. Why, she had a fine piece of cloth spread right out in the middle of the floor, and danged if she didn't put her foot right down on it! But I knowed better than to do anything like that and so managed to hop around and keep from stepping on it." [United States]

❧ Wheel and Spear ❧

Long, long ago, seven Cherokee Indian boys loved to play a game called Wheel and Spear. Because they neglected their chores in favor of playing more and more Wheel and Spear, their mothers became angry and gathered up their wheels and spears in the middle of the night while they were asleep. Then the mothers threw the spears and wheels in the pond near the Indian village.

In the morning when the boys awakened and discovered what had happened, they became so angry they decided to run away. They met at sunset at the pond. One boy played the drum while the others moved in a circle to the rhythm of the beat. As the drum beats grew faster and faster, the boys chanted as they danced. "We're going away and never return. We're going away and never return."

The drum beats, the chanting, and the boys' dance kept going faster and faster until the boys' feet raised right up off the ground. The mothers saw them and ran to catch them, but they were already spinning around too high for the mothers to reach them.

The seven boys spun around so high in the sky that they became seven dancing stars, and the Indians say that if you look at the sky on a clear night, you'll see them dancing still. [Native American]

How to Weigh an Elephant

A Chinese emperor received a gift of an elephant. He immediately wanted to know the weight of the elephant and commanded his ministers to solve the problem. If they could not tell him the weight in three days, they would lose their heads.

The ministers only had small scales, a thousand times too small to weigh the animal. By the third day, they were certain they were going to lose their heads.

Prince Chung, a young boy, announced on the third day that he could weigh the elephant. He put the elephant on a boat. Then he swam around the boat and marked the water line with red paint.

He removed the elephant and filled the boat with stones until the sides of the boat reached the previous water line. The boy then weighed the stones and added the weights together. He now knew the weight of the elephant.

Prince Chung, although a young boy, saved the heads of the ministers and became very popular with the emperor. [China]

The Lobster and the Crow

One day a crow, flying over the sea, spied a lobster below, swooped down, seized the lobster in his beak, and carried him off to the forest to enjoy eating him.

The lobster, knowing he was about to be gobbled up, said to the crow, "Crow, old chap, once upon a time I knew your mother and father. Fine people they were."

"Hm," grunted the crow. He didn't want to open his mouth to speak for fear he'd drop the lobster out of his beak.

"You know, I think I know your brothers and sisters, too," said the lobster. When he didn't get any reaction from the crow, he sort of gurgled, "Charming people!"

The lobster knew he had better hurry up and trick the crow into speaking or he was going to be an eaten lobster. With all the seductiveness he could muster, the lobster said, "I was just telling my lobster friends the other day that you come from the most charming, wise family I've ever met. And we decided that your family got their charm and wisdom from you."

"Really!" cried the crow, and because the lobster's flattery seduced him into opening his mouth, the crow lost his lunch to the sea. [Ukraine]

❧ How the Rainbow Came to Be ❧

One bright Summer day when the sun was warm and the breezes cool, the flowers nodded to show off their brilliant colors. A week before, only tulips as red as flame had danced in the wind. But now the whole garden was ignited with color. Already the butterflies had found the flowers and were dancing in and out and round about the blossoms, hoping for a sip of nectar.

In the middle of this abundant beauty, the Great Spirit heard one of the older flowers say to another, "I wonder where we will go when Winter comes. It doesn't seem fair to me. We do our share to make the Earth a beautiful place to live. Why shouldn't we have a happy hunting ground of our own?"

Frankly, the Great Spirit wasn't used to a flower having such a lengthy complaint. However, he considered what the flower had said. In fact, he thought about it quite a while. Finally, he announced, "Instead of the flowers dying when Winter arrives, I am going to have them provide the color for a rainbow."

That is why, after a refreshing shower, we are able to look up into the sky and see the beautiful, colored flowers of the past year making a beautiful rainbow across the heavens. [Native American]

✥ The Man Who Carried the Turkey ✥

In the early 1800s, an old man entered a meat market in Richmond, Virginia, and said to the butcher, "I would like a turkey." His coat was worn and his hat was dirty. When the butcher returned with a turkey for his inspection, the old man nodded, "Yes, my wife will like that one."

When the old man had left, a young man, dressed in fine clothes and carrying a shiny silver-handled cane, stepped up to the counter and said, "I would like a turkey similar to the one you sold to the old man."

The butcher asked, "Do you want it wrapped?"

The young man answered, "Yes," and handed the butcher the money. 'Please deliver it at once."

The butcher replied, "I cannot do that. We do not deliver."

"Well, then," said the young man, "how will I get it home?"

The butcher remained stone-faced and said, "Well, sir, I guess you will have to carry it."

"Carry it? Who do you think I am? I can't carry a turkey down the street." The young man looked very angry.

The old man who purchased the first turkey had stopped outside the door and heard everything that was said. He stepped inside and asked the young man, "Sir, would you tell me where you live?"

"Of course," said the young man. "I live at 39 Blank Street and my name is Johnson."

"Well, isn't that lucky," said the old man. "I happen to be going that way and would be glad to carry your turkey for you."

"Oh, yes!" said the young man, smiling. "Follow me."

When they reached Mr. Johnson's house, the old man handed over the turkey and turned to go.

"Wait," said the young man. "I must pay you something."

"Oh, no. You owe me nothing. It was no trouble," the old man answered, and then he turned and continued on his way.

The young Mr. Johnson was bewildered about why the old man had treated him so well. He was so curious about the man that he hurried back to the butcher to find out who he was.

"Oh, that's John Marshall, chief justice of the United States Supreme Court. He is one of the greatest men in our country. He just wanted to teach you a lesson."

The young man was already feeling ashamed, but he asked, "What was the lesson?"

"Oh, just that no one should feel that he is too good to carry his own packages."

"Oh, no!" said another man who had been in the market and had seen and heard everything. "Judge Marshall carried the turkey simply because he wished to be kind. That is his way."

❧ The Fearless One ❧

A young man was once bragging about how brave he was, saying, "You can send me to a haunted place. I won't be afraid." His friends took him up on his boast and led him to a graveyard. He was to stay there all night to prove that he was brave.

That night, the young man wore a large sweater that belonged to his father. It hung almost to his knees. He wore it because he knew it would become cold that night, and if his friends saw him shivering, they wouldn't think it was because of the temperature. They were sure to think he was shivering from fear.

The cemetery gate squeaked as he opened it. It was very dark. He couldn't see a light anywhere. The young man walked down the path a short way and sat down by a bush. It was a terrible darkness. He hadn't expected to feel as much fear as he did. But gradually he found his courage and went to sleep. In a short time, the hoot of an owl awakened him. His body went stiff with fear as he strained his ears to listen. The owl didn't hoot again. He figured it must have flown away, and he forced himself to relax. It was the only way to bring on sleep. Finally he dozed off, only to be awakened by the sound of footsteps! His heart pounded hard until he realized it was someone walking on the road outside the cemetery. Eventually, he did sleep soundly and didn't awaken until the early morning birds began to sing.

He smiled when he saw the dawn breaking. He'd won! They had said he couldn't do it. But he did! He wanted to run all the way home and tell them. But when he tried to get up, he couldn't. Something was holding him to the ground! "It's a ghost!" he screamed and fell back into a dead faint, where his friends found him a short time later.

Of course, it wasn't a ghost that had grabbed him, it was the bramblebush that his sweater was caught by. But he had fainted from fear! [Great Britain]

INDEX

ABOUT THE AUTHOR

Pat Nelson grew up in Minneapolis, Minnesota and learned about the magic of stories from her two grandmothers. Now a grandmother herself, she is also a professional storyteller based in Tulsa, Oklahoma. She is the co-founder of Reading & Arts for People (RAP) and artistic director of their annual storytelling festival. She has been a bookmobile librarian for the Tulsa City-County Library System and is a member of the National Association for Preservation and Perpetuation of Storytelling. Ms. Nelson is the former editor of the Tulsey Town Storyteller, a newsletter for storytellers. She holds a bachelor degree in Liberal Studies from Oklahoma University.